SUPERD

SUPERDOG!

Action plans that work for a happy and well-behaved pet

Chris Standen

Foreword by Katie Boyle

THORSONS PUBLISHING GROUP

First published 1990

© Chris Standen 1990

Illustrations by Chris Saunderson

British Library Cataloguing in Publication Data

Standen, Chris
Superdog!
1. Pets: Dogs. Training
I. Title
636.7'083

ISBN 0-7225-1741-6

Published by Thorsons Publishers Limited, Wellingborough, Northamptonshire, England NN8 2RQ

Typeset by Harper Phototypesetters Limited, Northampton, England
Printed and bound in Great Britain by Mackays of Chatham, Kent

Contents

Foreword

I can't remember a time when dogs weren't an intrinsic part of my life. My father had a talent for rescuing them from fates far worse than death in Italy, where I was born and bred, and it's a trait that I've inherited.

Rehabilitating traumatized pooches is becoming far more than a hobby for me — I have four of various shapes and sizes, which I call my Liquorice Allsorts, one mongrel, two small poodles and an Italian Greyhound — all refugees in one way and another from Battersea Dogs Home with which I've been closely and actively connected for over 20 years.

There is no doubt that an *understood* dog is much easier to train, and a well-trained dog is indeed a happy one — which certainly reflects on the family — or is it vice versa!?

Chris Standen, in *Superdog!*, aims to show us how to 'think dog'. This is so very important, because although we often tend and like to humanize our pets' reactions — 'he/she understands every word I say!' — the fact is that whether they be Rottweiler, poodle or mongrel-wrapped, they all share the *wolf* as their ancestor and, whatever we may wish to believe, their instincts do not always run parallel with ours.

In any field there are bound to be occasional differences in approach — as there are between Chris Standen and myself — however, I'm quite sure that readers of *Superdog!* will gain a tremendous amount of practical knowledge on which to build a sensibly caring relationship essential to having both a happy and well-behaved four-legged member of the family.

Katie Boyle

Introduction

Living with a dog

You will find this book different from other dog books.

I am, you see, a canine behavioural training consultant. That, in general terms, means that I am a consultant animal trainer who specializes in problem dogs, dogs whose behaviour makes their continuing life within a normal home impossible. They chew, bite, howl and fight their way to destruction or desertion.

In writing this book, I have looked at some of the more common problems and have illustrated them with a number of case histories from the files of Furdiths, my consultancy. Names, places, and breed are fictitious. The problems and cures however are genuine, and if you have a dog you may find that you relate closely to the people I'm writing about.

The dog

Man's best friend? After reading this book you may start to have second thoughts. Let us look at the object in front of the fire, and see if we can help you to understand why he or she does the things they do that so annoy you, frustrate you and make you look small in front of your friends.

It has been said that there is no such thing as a bad dog, only a bad owner. This may not be strictly true, but it is as good a place as any at which to start.

There *are* bad owners as indeed there are bad dogs, but it is more often the case that the owner is just badly educated.

Man's best friend has, over the years, been taken for granted — 'It's only a dog' is a well-worn cliché — but a more worrying tendency which has begun to develop recently is for dog owners to treat their pets less as companions and more as status symbols.

Have you ever played 'match the dog to the person'? I do it regularly — Mrs Whatnot looks like somebody who should own an Afghan, etc.

To take the game a little further, Mr Macho would probably own a Rottweiler, Dobermann, or (if out of touch) a German Shepherd. He is to be seen in most parks. His dog is usually chasing yours, or walking loose along the road. There are two explanations for this. In the first place, it is definitely uncool to scream at your dog, so he will make no attempt to control it preferring to laugh it off and walk away instead. Secondly, he has no desire to be seen being pulled along by a huge dog — what a blow that would be for his image! It is far easier to let the dog off its lead on the main road and pretend you have trained it to walk 20 yards ahead of you and wait for you at kerbs.

Mr Macho is blind to all his problems. He thinks it is funny if his dog attacks people (again he pretends it is trained to do so) and he doesn't hear the pleas of his wife who can't cope with a dog which growls at her when he is out.

Mr Macho

This kind of attitude has resulted in certain breeds being branded as bad — the three types of dog mentioned above are obvious examples. People tend to forget the very steady, devoted police and military dogs which these animals make. No one could accuse these dogs of being mad.

Our second victim is the much acclaimed yuppie. Match him or her with a Springer Spaniel, Labrador, Weimaraner or even a pointer or setter. His or her problems are quite different. They have working dogs in order to show them off at weekends together with their green wellies, wax jackets, flat caps, and riding gloves. They live the life of the commuter and expect the dog to respond like a clockwork toy. There's no time in their busy schedule for walking the dog, except to

Mr Yuppie

clear Saturday's hangover in time for Sunday lunch. While Mr and Mrs Yuppie are at work from nine to five plus travel, their little baby chews the home to pieces with frustration and for the want of a good walk. It is also the scourge of the local farmer — once let off the lead, it rarely returns until it wants to, but chases everything in sight, trying to run off a little steam. Mr and Mrs Yuppie acknowledge their problem but blame bad breeding. They usually make the excuse that they simply haven't the time to correct it, and tend to prefer rehousing the dog and starting again.

And what about Mr and Mrs Small Dog? Little dog is totally psychopathic, thrashing across the park on its extending lead and body harness with its owner acting as an anchor trying desperately to look calm, collected, and in control; but secretly, he or she knows full well that if let off the lead the small kamikaze would be gone. This dog breaks all the rules, goes to its owner's bed, sits on laps, eats chocolate, and watches TV but in their eyes he can do no wrong. He's just a little misunderstood, that's all!

Fortunately many dog owners do not fit into these cate-

This dog breaks all the rules . . .

gories and the majority of people own a dog for companionship and are quite keen to keep it under control.

In the following chapters I intend to take you through some of the problems our best friend causes us, using case histories from our own records — you may well see yourself and your dog described! If you do then perhaps these stories might give you some help in dealing with your animal's problems.

Remember though that all conditions need individual consideration and will certainly require more detailed attention than I could give them in any book. Yet, if by reading through the disasters and laughing at them or shedding a tear you have been helped towards understanding your dog a little better, I will have succeeded.

Chapter 1

The early months

Before getting a dog it is a good idea to consider all aspects of the responsibility you are taking on.

Making the decision

What type of dog should we get?

To find the answer to this first important question, ask yourself: How large is our house, and how much space do we need?

Select the room your dog is most likely to spend its nights in (please don't say the bedroom). Ideally it will be a utility room or kitchen. Check that it is dry, secure, easily cleanable and well ventilated but not draughty. Remember your new dog may be messy, so the room is better not carpeted. When you have checked it for these points, make sure that nobody can see you and get down on hands and knees and turn round quickly in a full circle. If you knock against things or cannot turn around properly, repeat the process with a smaller human 'guinea-pig'. When you find a member of the family that can turn around without any difficulty use them as your measure. Given that a person's legs protrude when they are on their hands and knees, you should be looking for a dog two-thirds the length of your rotating 'guinea-pig'. This will also ensure that your dog has ample space to pace around in. To double check that this estimated size is not too big for the rest of the house, take your dog impersonator into your main living area and repeat the exercise. If he or she doesn't look too cramped there, then you have your size.

Do we want our dog indoors?

I must admit to condoning the use of kennels for dogs. I am not saying that your dog should stay there all of the time, but as a bedroom, a well-built kennel can be a great boon socially — although they spend the days with me, both my dogs have their kennel to go off and sleep in at night. They go there of their own accord when the kids get noisy or when they just want a cosy nap. What is more, if you are called away for an emergency or go out on a day trip, putting your dog in its kennel will mean that you don't have to worry about having to get home in case the dog messes.

A well-built kennel will be insulated, dry, warm, well ventilated, secure and safe with no sharp corners, and ideally should be built over a drain for easy cleaning. It will also always have a run.

Are we house-proud?

This question must be answered honestly. A dog will almost always cause disruption to your organized lives. Dog hairs on the carpet will mean more regular cleaning and how will you react to the odd flea popping onto your guests' arms during a visit? Could you cope if the dog vomited on your best rug or knocked over your pot plants and ornaments with his tail? What about those muddy paws crossing the newly washed floor or that lovely cream-coloured carpet?

Young puppies love to chew. What a talking point those teethmarks on the dining table legs and the scratches up the back door will be!

If you like your home 'just so' then you should not even consider having a dog of any kind.

How much does it all cost?

Initial outlay for dog owners could be quite sizeable. A pedigree dog will never cost less than a three-figure sum (unless it is unwanted and has problems) and fashionable breeds often fall into the four-figure price bracket!

You will need some basic equipment, at least three sizes of collar to allow for growth in the first year, a strong lead, two bowls — one for food, the other for water — a bed — preferably chew-proof — a lining for the bed and a brush and a comb for daily grooming and cleanliness.

A medium-sized dog will devour at least one can of food plus biscuits per day (or the equivalent in dry food). The bill for this alone can be quite surprisingly high worked out over the year. Your young puppy will eat a great deal more and need quite a few more expensive accessories than an adult dog.

Then there are those little extras, such as regular supplies of parasitical powder, shampoo, conditioning tablets and treats (the odd special bone or chew).

However, probably your biggest outlay will be in vets' bills. In the first week or so you will have to take your puppy for a health check (most vets charge a consultation fee). Then, at 12–14 weeks, he will have to be vaccinated against hardpad, distemper, leptospirosis and parvovirus. In today's over-crowded canine society, those vaccinations are expensive and absolutely necessary. They also need to be carried out every year.

If you are sensible, you'll get a good insurance policy. The annual premium can be a little steep, but will be well worth it if your dog is injured. Then there are those little incidentals: the routine veterinary bills for worming, the new fence to keep Rover from bothering the neighbours and so on.

As I have said before the responsible owner will also arrange spaying or neutering to keep their dog puppy-free. This can be a very expensive business but remember that the cost of rearing accidental conceptions could be even higher.

Holidays have to be considered too. The cost of boarding Rover while you go off to sun yourself on the Costa del Sol could be enough to encourage you to stay in the Costa del backyard!

Taking your dog on holiday with you can also involve extra expense. Anyone catering for pets will have covered for this by increasing the price of the holiday.

I haven't quoted definite prices for the items mentioned because they vary so much, but for an average wage-earning family, the cost could be considerable.

So, it is going to be expensive. If you are a gambler, you could cut corners — but who wants to gamble with the life of a friend?

Have we the time to look after it properly?

Not only the time, but the energy. The answer in many cases is no. Being humans we tend to overlook this point. But remember the puppy. You create the foundation for its future.

A puppy has special needs. When you get it home, it will whimper about, eat and sleep a lot, play with things and make the occasional rush to the garden to divert a piddle from the carpet. These first few weeks will be tiring for you but at least you will be warm — you won't have to go out very much at all and the newspaper on the floor means you can sleep in on occasions. But this stage passes quickly. Before long, walks will have to be taken — long ones, in the rain and snow. Training starts — frustrating periods of running about in fields chasing the wayward pup, getting up early, forcing back that warm quilt on a cold winter's morning, rushing to the shops to get the dog food you forgot, oh what fun! The hidden message here is, make sure you can cope with the commitment.

Exercise is important for both moral and practical reasons. If your dog lacks exercise, it could start to become frustrated. This will lead to destructive behaviour or bad house-training. Your dog is also likely to become obese and unhealthy. This will increase your vet's bills and shorten your companion's life. Finally, the dog is a prisoner, albeit a well-kept one, dependent on you to open the cell, prepare the food, slop him out and exercise him — YOU ARE HIS WARDER. I would suggest a minimum of two walks a day, each of no less than 30 minutes. The garden, no matter how big, is boring and is only for wandering around in in-between times.

How does a dog affect your social life?

Simple — considerably! I would compare the arrival of a dog to suddenly finding you have a baby to look after.

Consider your friends. Is there someone close to you who does not like dogs? Single people, especially the young, should consider what would happen if a new human relationship is started. How would the dog accept this? Young couples need to think what would happen if they have a child. Remember, the dog could well be with you for 15 years or so.

Holidays, sun, sand, sea — but where do you put the dog? Is it to go to a kennel? If so, book early. Is someone going to dog-sit for you? The dog may not like them.

Bear in mind too that you cannot go abroad with *any* animal. If you settle for a holiday at home, remember not to take the dog out with you in the car for the day, if it is hot. It will die if it overheats too much, even if it isn't sunny. If you do take it, leave some windows open.

The social scene on holiday is usually fun but, of course, you wouldn't know, because you can't take the dog to the restaurant, the disco, theatre or cinema but you can't leave it in the hotel either, it may howl.

So, self-catering and perhaps braving the unpredictable weather may be your only choice!

I'm afraid I've painted a rather bleak picture. I do believe dogs are good for people but they fit in only if you do some planning first.

What will the neighbours think?

If you are responsible and have proper fences, ensure that your dog is quiet and minds its manners, I foresee no problem. But if you ignore the neighbours' feelings, you will find yourself in trouble. 'Noise pollution' can land you in court and could even mean the end of your dog. So please consult them and encourage them to enjoy your dog instead of giving them cause to complain about it.

What about our age?

For a retired person, a dog can be a wonderful tonic to help fill the gap left by work. However, a young dog can be exceedingly demanding and sometimes very frustrating. The over-sixties should think carefully about this. Consider the state of your back and your overall fitness. If you are thinking of getting a dog after your retirement, choose one of light frame which will not be too energetic. Do not be drawn into the trap of having that German Shepherd you always wanted. Smaller breeds make just as good if not better companions.

If you are 65 or over you should try to think long term. Unlike us, dogs on the whole stay active a lot longer, at 11 and 12 years old some dogs are still as energetic as they were when they were five.

A 15-year lifespan is not uncommon for a dog. By this time you will be 80 years old or thereabouts. I like to believe that at that age I will still be running down to the post office. However, in reality there is every chance I will be Grumpy Grandpa, who can't get about very much and relies on meals on wheels. I am not for a moment suggesting that senior citizens should not own dogs, but consider the matter carefully before you make a decision. Don't forget that the hardest dogs to find homes for are those over seven years old. If you find that you genuinely need a companion at the age of 70, then perhaps one of these friends, already housetrained and in their twilight years, may be just the job?

Another possibility might be a cat. They do not need to be taken for walks. I have six, which may be a little extreme, but they can show just as much love and affection towards their owners as dogs. Besides, you can't sit with a Great Dane on your lap for an evening, can you?

Exercise areas — where are they?

How far is your nearest open space? Once you have found it, can you use it? There has recently been a rapid increase in restrictions on dog fouling.

It is an offence to let your dog foul a footpath, and always has been. Many more people are now reporting offenders when they spot them. The fine can be quite high and the offence can get you mentioned in the papers. Away from open spaces, it is your duty to pick up your dog's faeces. When you get to your park you will probably find the same thing applies here. You may not be allowed in with a dog at all or a pick-it-up campaign could be in force. Dog owners have always considered that open spaces belong to them, but thankfully, things have now changed. So if you don't want to accept the responsibility of cleaning up after your animal, don't put yourself in a position where you might have to.

Country dwellers with easy access to all those fields seem, at first glance, to be living in a dog's paradise. But once again it is not as simple as it appears. Farmers don't need much prompting to tell you that 'damn dog owners' are the scourge of their lives. Many will then chase you off their land quite aggressively. Claiming that you are on a public footpath is no defence, unless your dog is on a lead. It is an offence for your dog to be in a field with livestock. Even if he never chases the animals, it could get him shot — and you prosecuted.

The dog-owning public really have only themselves to blame for such drastic measures. After all, farmers are only protecting their livelihoods. How many of us have complained bitterly if a stray dog comes into our garden and fouls before going on its way? Dogs must be controlled, regardless of the environment.

So, whether in a rural or an urban setting, find out the facts. Read the by-laws. In towns, find out what the rules are before you decide to get a dog. In the country, ask before you trespass. Many farmers will tell you which fields to avoid and which to enter. I know of one who places a marker on the gates to show the locals where they can enter safely and this is widely appreciated.

Choosing your new friend

Now you have answered the questions and have satisfied yourself that you do genuinely need a dog, you must face the rigours of selecting one. Set your sights on exactly what you require. We all have favourites and I would be foolish to try to tell you what dog you need. But be sure you know what you are looking for. It is always a bit hit and miss as to whether you will end up getting just what you want but in the next few pages I will try to point you in the right direction.

The pedigree dog

If you want a pedigree dog you will need to keep your wits about you. As with any market, there are reputable people and disreputable ones who will be ready to sell you anything at the highest price they can possibly get.

A few words of advice. Never purchase from friends. If the dog doesn't come up to expectations, you will feel that you won't be able to complain because of your friendship and you will probably never feel that he is quite yours. Whenever your friends visit, little comments like 'How's our little baby then?' or 'His mother was twice the dog that this one is' can be very hurtful. The friendship is bound to suffer under the strain.

Never purchase a dog from the small ads in the newspaper. The local paper is the hunting ground of many a disreputable 'hobby breeder'. These are people who insist on letting their dogs have a litter of pups. They usually operate on the promise that 'so-and-so's dog along the street is the same breed, so let's get together'. Their reasons may be harmless, but money — that little extra for Christmas — is the key.

This haphazard method can spell disaster for you. A dog breeder should know everything there is to know about their particular breed in case things go wrong, and should be able to furnish you with a brief history of not only the breed in general, but the breed line that they are using. If you have problems with your dog early on, the breeder should be able to give you advice and guidance. I am not saying that breeders should be able to answer major headaches; that is for the veterinary surgeon or consultants like myself to deal with. However, they should be able to help with little problems like what to feed the dog, how to brush it and what faults are common to the breed.

The hobby breeder is generally no more qualified than you

in 'doggy' matters except that they have owned a dog long enough to get it pregnant, and if you get your dog from such a source, you could find yourself adrift with no reference point whatsoever when the chips are down.

The professional dog breeder is also out to make money, but, hopefully, they will be able to provide a back-up service. They must, at any event, have a licence from the local authority. This is the first thing that you should ask to see. The licence is issued under the Boarding and Breeding of Dogs Act 1900, which basically sets out standards of cleanliness and hygiene as well as stating minimum requirements for the dogs' well-being. This licence is renewed annually and if the breeder fails to come up to standard, the licence is revoked. So if the person you decide to purchase from is unlicensed, you should tread carefully.

The next step is to find out exactly what after-care your prospective breeders are going to give you and to check their reputation. Ask around, go and see them informally before you decide and see what sort of impression you get from meeting them. If you find them unapproachable, leave them alone. Don't be ashamed or frightened to say thanks, but no thanks. As business people they should be able to respect your views.

When you have made up your mind, make sure any agreement you make is in writing. These days, word of mouth is never to be accepted. Remember, a salesman is usually very courteous when selling, but rarely so nice if you have a complaint to make. If people are unwilling to commit their promises to paper, you should refuse to take the dog.

Like any other commodity, pedigree dogs are covered by the Sale of Goods Act. If your dog does not satisfy the needs for which it was purchased, then the seller of the dog is legally bound to refund your money, replace the dog or pay for you to have the problem corrected for the first 12 months. Obviously this does not apply to all problems, but if you have a dog as a family pet and, for example, it bites your children without provocation or it won't stop chewing your house to pieces, then it is obviously not suited to life as a pet. A good breeder will know this, so ensure that it is written into your contract.

Be sure of getting the dog you want. Don't put your name to something as yet unborn. When you go to choose, if a bitch is what you want, then look only at bitches. Please do not be bulldozed into accepting the one remaining dog if all the bitches have been spoken for. And don't listen to such remarks as 'If he doesn't go, we'll have to have him put down'. That is the breeder's problem and, quite frankly, it's something that they should have considered when the dog was mated. (It may even be untrue.) A good breeder would have no need to resort to such tactics in the first place.

Another thing to watch out for is the slightly older dog which the breeder will offer to let you have at a reduced price. This is often a dog left over from the last litter, or one that has been out to a home and been returned because of some complaint. Think carefully. If it is five months old and living in a kennel, it will have many faults that a novice could not cope with.

Beware also of the slightly imperfect dog. Never consider an animal with a defect, such as an overshot or an undershot jaw where the top teeth do not align properly with the bottom ones and vice versa. The complaint can cause problems for the dog when eating and drinking.

Another big problem associated with pedigrees is hip dysplasia. Many breeds now suffer from this complaint, but truly reputable dog breeders will ensure that it is eventually bred out. For your peace of mind, ensure that the breeder you use can guarantee a hip score programme. This is a system where breeding dogs are X-rayed by a veterinary surgeon and awarded a score for the condition of the hip joint. *Only* use a breeder who is aware of this process and is using it. I have met many breeders and people advertising themselves as breeders who have said 'A hip what?'.

Any breeder you select should understand the breed, be able and willing to advise on minor matters, provide an after-sale service and be willing to take responsibility should things go wrong. If they won't — don't use them.

Selecting a mongrel

The most resilient dog in the world and, I believe, the most faithful companion, is the good old cur. Choosing one can be fun. Puppies are always a gamble, but if you want an adult dog, keep looking and you will eventually find one that suits you.

There are a few ground rules, however. Put your emotions away and don't take them out until you get home again. The world of the animal sanctuary is one of much heartbreak and despair. It was quoted to me recently that in Britain 5,000 dogs are destroyed every day. If you can't find a suitable four-legged friend from amongst this vast army of dogs, then something is not quite right.

As to actual selection, choose your sanctuary carefully. Some are better equipped and more professional than others. Only go to a sanctuary that looks and smells clean. (Many are charities, so don't pay attention to actual building structure.) Find out how the sanctuary operates and, as with breeders, go and investigate first. Drop in and chat to the person in charge; preferably use a sanctuary that insists on visiting your home to check that you are suitable. Go in with your eyes open. If you have a preference to sex or age, stick to it. Never mind little Joey who is due to be put down tomorrow — he will be joined by 2,000 others and is, unfortunately, just one of many.

Try to use a sanctuary that has a compulsory neuter/spay policy since this shows that they have a responsible attitude to fighting the problem of strays and are not just concerned with passing them on. Insist on a file history of the animal you are interested in. In some cases this is not possible, as for example when a dog has been picked up as a stray. However, it should be available if the dog you are interested in has been brought in by its previous owners.

If it has been dumped by its owners, make sure you know why. It could be that they couldn't afford it or haven't the time for a dog any more, but equally it could be that it is very destructive or picks fights with other dogs. If you cannot obtain any background information then ask for a report on its kennel behaviour. All sanctuaries keep dogs for seven days to see if they are claimed before offering them for adoption. Find out how it has behaved. Again, check what after-care service is available. I regularly take referrals from sanctuaries that recognize the responsibilities of adopting a dog and use our service if there are problems that they cannot cope with.

Once you are happy with the set-up, you may want to let the sanctuary staff help in the selection process. The RSPCA (Royal Society for the Prevention of Cruelty to Animals) adoption system, which requires you to answer some very detailed questions, is to be commended. In this way, they can get a good idea (if you are honest) of what type of dog would be best suited to you. Together you can discuss the possibilities and draw up a shortlist from which to make your selection. From then on it's up to you.

I like to see character in a dog; looks mean little if one takes your fancy. Ask if you can take it out for a walk — if not, why not? — just to see how you get on. If you think the dog isn't for you then say so. The staff will respect your honesty and always prefer an honest 'no' to getting the dog back from you after a short period and everyone ending up unhappy. Don't be afraid to ask questions. If it's 'yes' to the dog, express your opinions to the staff, let them take him back to his kennel and go home. Sleep on it and talk about it. You may find one member of the family is not so keen, but was afraid to say so at the time. Go back the next day to decide. Remember, you are never honour bound to take an animal just because you liked it the first time around. Repeat the process. Take it for another walk and see if you still feel the same about it. If you do, then decide; if your feelings have changed, walk away. You will probably find that the sanctuary staff will advise you to do this anyway. When you are given the dog to take home with you will depend greatly on their policy. They may withhold the dog until they have checked you out. This is normal and only fair, and you should always respect their decision in such matters.

When you get home

Your dog will be between eight and ten weeks old when you get it home. Extreme patience at this time is essential. I believe very strongly that how your adult dog turns out is decided in these next crucial months. The puppy had just left the security and comfort of his own family group. Everything he had come to recognize in his short life has suddenly changed. His strongest sense — smell — will be confused. The smell of your home, his brand new bed and even your distinct human odour will be completely alien to him. He must learn to accept you as you must learn to accept him.

His first reaction to all this will probably be to do a puddle. In his confused state this is to be expected. We would probably do the same! Don't get angry, it's no big deal and can be avoided by taking a few simple precautions. Don't let the whole family grab and fondle the new dog as soon as he arrives. Instead, have his new bed prepared ready for his arrival. In it, place various items that were worn by the family, your old jumper, the kids' old vest. Try to include one for every member of the family, and make sure that they have been worn and are not freshly washed. This will allow the dog to familiarize himself with your personal smells during the quieter moments.

Before you put him to bed, place him on the area that you want him to urinate on. Personally, I favour bio-degradable cat litter. There are also some good compressed natural woodchip varieties on the market. Once he has been to the little dog's room, put the litter tray in his pen with him. That way if he is up and exploring he will, in theory, stumble on the familiar smell and use the litter tray again.

During his first day leave him alone for a few quiet periods of about an hour each. Listen out for serious cries of distress but where possible ignore him, he will soon settle down. If you think logically about it, this time when he is alone is not greater than the time he would have to spend on his own whilst his natural mother was away, either finding food or going about her own business. When you or the family return to him be steady in your movements, use your hands firmly to stroke him in his bed area, and when you have finished, leave him without getting him excited.

The first night don't feed him until after the kids, or whoever, have cuddled him. Once fed, tuck him in for the night and then leave him. Do not keep popping back because he is upset or howling. It is essential that he learns your

Superdog!

routine as soon as possible. This fretting will probably continue for two to three days.

The next step, once your new arrival has settled in, is a trip to your chosen veterinary surgeon. The sooner the dog's vaccination programme starts, the sooner he can start going out into the big world.

When he is between 8 and 15 weeks old, the dog is at his most receptive not in terms of training but with regard to his perception of the world. Confidence can be built during this time — and easily broken. Fears and phobias can be picked up but if you are a confident, steady owner, the dog can be subconsciously schooled to accept many things totally alien to him.

Firstly, you must avoid adjusting your own voice tones too much. Keep yourself calm and keep your manner towards the puppy firm, but not loud or over-excited. People who use their voice loudly or excitedly could project their own fears. You must be seen as a leader to be both fair and confident as a parent should be. To suddenly run towards a small dog shouting 'Bad dog, bad dog' in your loudest tone will make him cringe.

He may stop nibbling the telephone cord but it can cause an over-the-top reaction and as a result the dog often forgets the lesson. Approaching the dog, tapping him on the nose or giving him a firm shake on the scruff of his neck and saying 'no', will have some effect, and is a lot less traumatic for the dog. Little things that are everyday noises to you could affect your puppy. The vacuum cleaner may be a daily noise to you, but to a new puppy it could be a monster. So, take precautions. Start upstairs, so that the noise is less loud and leave the door open so that the dog can come and have a look. If he becomes distressed then act as the brave leader. Leave the hoover running, go to the dog and stroke him in your normal fashion, then let him see you go back to the hoover and carry on. The puppy may not follow you but he can see that you are not afraid so there is nothing to concern him. Do not, however, keep going back for a cuddle or try to force a meeting with the hoover by tucking the puppy under your arm and carrying him to confront the monster, this will only promote fear.

The new dog will be very inquisitive, so be patient with him. He will invariably knock things over and after the first few days become prone to fits of playing madly for short periods, so protect your valuables in the same way as you would if there was a toddler in the house. Remove obvious breakables or items of danger from ground level. This must include household cleaning materials, many of which can cause real discomfort, and can even be fatal to the animal. Pot plants are another very often ignored danger. Apart from causing a mess when they are knocked over, a great many houseplants are extremely toxic and poisonous to animals. They may not have a lasting effect but they can make a dog feel thoroughly uncomfortable.

Keep playtime calm. The puppy will be quite capable of dashing about and performing in front of you but join in only on an acceptable level. You don't have to get down on all fours and do the same. If you roughhouse, then the puppy will respond by using his mouth and as he becomes more power-ful and confident, this can become extremely painful for you. It is also something which is difficult to stop the animal from doing when he gets bigger. Games such as tug of war should also be avoided. It may be fun to grab hold of one end of a piece of cloth and pull it about but this will create problems later. You and your family must be able to take things from the dog and it is extremely unfair to suddenly start scolding him at 6 months old because he won't give up something that was once his to play with.

Give him a solid ball which you can roll for him. Once again, however, don't let this become a repeated habit. Don't persist in the game every time the dog comes to you. Some-times, just ignore the item and stroke the dog.

I believe that toys should be kept to a minimum, and should be very carefully selected. I tend to avoid any toy with a squeak in it, for several reasons. Firstly this type of toy is normally copied from the toys that young children play with, and this can lead to trouble if the dog steals a child's toy in error. This is easily done, because the dog is attracted by smell. The smell of sticky biscuits as well! Secondly, such toys usually have to be bitten before they will squeak. The noise which they produce is very similar to that which a distressed baby can make and I have known cases where dogs have nipped babies in order to achieve the same sound.

Avoid at all costs toys made from old personal belongings. To the dog, the chewy old shoe smells exactly the same as your best work one, and it is you, after all, who has allowed him to relate to these smells. Remember too that a knotted sock is the same as one from the wash basket. This could well encourage your dog to start attacking your washing at some point in the future. Most importantly, these sorts of toys smell of you, your deodorant, work, body odour, washing powder, and if the toys are not available to the dog, then he may go for any object identifiable by the same smell, sofas, stools, jumpers, carpets and so on.

I prefer natural objects, my favourite being a length of raw beef shin bone about two inches long initially with the marrow removed (to prevent a runny tummy) and cut off at the end to make a ring. Failing this, a plain hide bone from the pet shop will do, but don't confuse this with coloured chewable sticks. A hide chew is off-white in colour, a little smelly and lasts ages whereas the coloured sticks fragment and last only a few minutes.

Taking your puppy out

You cannot really start going out until your dog has completed his vaccination programme, but you can still teach him a few lessons. Choose a place in your garden for his outdoor toilet, and from time to time place the initial litter tray deposits over this area. This will help the dog decide where to go in later months. If you are tempted to take him out on the streets before then you are taking a gamble.

I see many people carrying their new puppy about with them, but this is no safeguard against the dangerous viruses which may affect him because these can be airborne. If you go into environments already used by dogs you could infect the puppy, whether you are carrying him or letting him walk. Simply by visiting other dog owners, you could become a source of infection. Veterinary surgeons recommend that you keep the dog in to minimize the risk and it's advice which should be followed.

Once you have got the all clear to take your dog out, it's time to start schooling the puppy into a more working routine, namely taking walks for exercise. This must be done at a pace that the dog can accept. The first few runs out are always traumatic. It's a whole new world full of smells, noises, objects, sights and sounds which the puppy has never before encountered. He may sit down and refuse to move, pull headlong into the nearest wall or just run amok. One thing is certain, he will probably rebel against the new collar and lead that has been put on him, so make sure that he has been accustomed to these beforehand. He should wear the collar all the time in these early days.

Your attitude again counts for a lot. You set the pace at all times. On the first few occasions when you take him out choose somewhere that is reasonably close to home, a park for example or a friendly farmer's field. Pick a place where the dog can become fully absorbed in all the smells. Remember too on these expeditions that you are the leader and show that you are confident so that he will turn to you to allay his fears. However, you must try to avoid over-protective behaviour and you should certainly never bully your dog into doing anything he doesn't want to do.

You can start more advanced training after that crucial first week. The important point to note is that you must not show apprehension when you are out. This is not as easy as it seems. Dogs tend to interpret your actions a little differently from the way in which you would expect them to. For instance, if you walk past a loud or unusual noise and the dog stops or pulls away (car exhausts are the classic example) it is only natural to want to give comfort and reassurance — but this could be disastrous. If you run away as well, the dog will think that you are as frightened as he is. Instead, you could do one of several things. For example you could keep walking regardless and then praise the dog: he has passed the object of his fear. Alternatively, you could hold your ground until the dog calms down, then steadily but firmly pull him to you and make a game of it by stroking him, talking normally and walking on while you have his attention. Either one of these approaches to the problem should ensure that you pass the object without making a big show of things.

When people approach you, the dog will react in one of two ways. He is most likely to dash along and leap all over them. If he does this, you should keep walking, firmly say 'no' and pull him away. The second reaction, less common but more frustrating, is for the dog to pull away and sit down. It's a problem which is relatively easy to beat. Either let the person stop, bend down and stroke your dog before they continue on their way or stop the person yourself and try to strike up a conversation with them. After a few seconds the dog, if he is being ignored, will come forward to investigate. Stroke him casually and then walk on. When you get to the park let him have a good run about straight away. Tie him on to a long length of line and hold the other end, that way you can't lose him. The exercise will be good for him and you are letting him gain confidence for himself yet at the same time providing him with a safety net in case he gets into trouble.

At this stage I must admit to disagreeing with most dog trainers. I believe in teaching the recall commands as soon as possible. The sooner the dog gets to run loose, safely and under control, the better. I dispute the need to keep a dog on the lead and to give him only light exercise sessions until he has reached 6 months. This is certainly not what would happen in the natural world. Exercise is essential to build strong muscles and so if exercise is dangerous to them then dogs must obviously have been bred with a defect. The excuse for this restriction was given to me recently by a breeder of Great Danes. He believed that a Great Dane's heart was too small for its body until it started growing at six months old — and he was a professional! It could reasonably be argued that since so many dogs suffer disorders of the hips, a programme of light exercise in the first few months might reduce the chances of such a problem being discovered. I have always been of the opinion that, rather like young children, dogs have a built-in safety mechanism that prevents them from doing things that are over-strenuous. This only goes wrong when we adults try to hurry things along, or encourage our little protégés to reach greater heights more quickly then they want to.

A few tips for these first few weeks then:

- Be confident and patient.

- Set a standard and stick to it.

- Go to places that are quieter than normal (not main roads).

- Tackle one new experience at a time.

- Keep your command words simple, repetitive and quiet.

- Do not get annoyed.

- Do not be embarrassed by your animal in public.

- Remember, the dog is a living thing. Don't show off with him for your own amusement.

- Introduce him steadily to the family.

- Do not make him the centre of your life and then drop him later.

- Do not take chances with his health.

5 months and onward

If you have stayed the course this long you will find that your chosen companion is rapidly becoming the dog that you have been waiting for. Over the months that follow, he will grow and take shape and changes will start to take place in his character. I always think of this stage as the time when problems that you may be encountering need sorting out. Judging from the number of calls I receive after Christmas, when the novelty of a new puppy is wearing off, this certainly appears to be the case. The dog is still very young and does stupid things, but at this stage his owners no longer see him as a puppy.

Chewing problems are possibly the most prevalent. The change to adult teeth is well advanced and it is now that the habits, good or bad, are either dealt with or reinforced. We have already covered the areas that reinforce them but to prevent them is equally simple. The dog has a never-ending thirst for knowledge, and we can use this to our advantage.

Now is the ideal time to step up the control training.

Teach your dog some basic commands, not 'sit for a biscuit' or anything as mundane as that, but lessons that will make your life easier. When you go out, teach him not to sniff, or teach him to walk to 'heel'. If he likes to chase a ball, don't just throw it for him in the park, hide it. Let him see you hide it in several places then encourage him to find it. It's up to you to keep the dog occupied.

When you have to leave the dog alone for a while give him a juicy bone to chomp so that his attention is diverted from the table legs! If he does start to damage the furniture or furnishings then sprinkle it with something which tastes unpleasant — I have always found alum salt in solution ideal.

When the dog is 6 months old, you can adjust his feeding routine. I suggest that one feed per day is enough for all dogs around the home. Remember that the feeding guide given by manufacturers applies to active dogs. In practice, most dogs will require a lot less than the manufacturer's recommended amount. I have deliberately not gone into detail on this topic because the amount which your dog will require will depend on its size and the life it leads, but if you want guidance on this matter you can always ask your vet or contact someone like myself.

The owner of a female dog must now start making a serious effort to save up for a spaying as the next problem you will have to face if you have a bitch, will be the 'season'. This is a traumatic time for any young lady dog. 'Season' or 'oestrus' refers to the development of the female parts and to the time when roughly every six months or so, unless she is spayed, all the male suitors in the neighbourhood will be interested in mating with her. This lasts three weeks and if you are very observant you'll know when to expect it. Normally it is preceded by the dog squatting to urinate a little more frequently than normal.

It is essential that you take every precaution during this time to keep the boys away, even if it means driving out in the car to secluded fields to give your dog a walk on the lead. Never let her off the lead as you never know what lusty thought may spring into her mind! Secluded spots are best because apart from the fact that if you walk her in a park or on the road, you will run the risk of confrontation with male dogs, you must also think of the frustration that your female will cause to the dogs that use these areas. They will smell her smells and could become unsettled and upset.

The owner of a male dog should also start putting some money aside for castration. In this way, in future, the dog need not be upset by the smells that it meets. At 8 months old, the leg cocking starts. Castration is an obvious way of preventing the male problems that are associated with this and which include marking furniture and door frames with urine and mounting visitors' legs when the dog becomes excited. Both spaying and castration can involve heavy bills if they are not prepared for and, believe me, both are well worth saving for as I hope I have shown. With over 50,000 stray and unwanted dogs roaming the streets of Britain surely it would be best to take steps to avoid adding to the problem.

Learning together

Body language is of immense importance when working with dogs. The poses we adopt towards our dogs will be interpreted by them in a number of ways and influence the way a dog develops.

Let us look at a few common body language moves on both sides and put them together to show what they can lead to, especially in young animals.

The classic 'play bow' is essentially a dog's signal that it wants to play. The front paws are thrust out, hind quarters elevated and the dog seems agitated. He then starts barking or grumbling. When approached he will dart off in a circle and normally returns to re-adopt the pose until his partner joins in this play; a game of chase follows.

We have all seen dogs do it. The owner tends to react by patting his knees, bending over, and making a grab.

Notice anything familiar in this behaviour? With arms outstretched, hind quarters raised, becoming excited (exasperated), barking (frustrated words in garbled sentences), and eventually having to resort to running after the dog, the owner is telling him that they want to play too!

The 'play bow'

The owner is telling him that he wants to play too!

The aggressive stance

Our second pose is the aggressive stance: dog rigid, ears back, teeth bared. Is there a human counterpart? I believe so — scolding — the human tendency to get angry to the extreme. Here too with rigid body, grimacing face, pointed finger, low angry voice and fixed stare, the owner is again mimicking the dog's behaviour.

What about the submissive stance where the dog sidles up, keeping very low to the ground, tail down, often whimpering and rolls over exposing his belly to the dominant party?

For a human equivalent, take the way in which somebody would try to tackle a frightened dog or a very aggressive dog, crouching down, sidling up, offering words of quiet encouragement (mostly for their own sake), all the time hesitant and slow, never quite wanting to touch the dog in case he bites but letting him sniff their hands.

Striking with a paw for attention is another doggy signal for play. Normally the dog paws the back of its mate and this leads to a quick rough and tumble on the ground until their

The human counterpart

attention is attracted elsewhere. The equivalent human response consists of pushing the dog away when you are sitting on the floor for example or trying to mend the car. This may be intended as a shove of rejection but unfortunately it usually has totally the opposite effect. The dog then leaps all over you; you push him off again and you both end up tussling on the floor until someone comes in and breaks it up.

These are just some of the very common human reactions which appear to duplicate a dog's behaviour and which, if they are interpreted wrongly by our animals can get us off to

The submissive stance

Tackling a frightened dog

the wrong start, leading us to believe that we have a wayward or troublesome dog on our hands. What is more, there are many more poses, far more subtle than these which can also give off the wrong signals. The only advice I can offer on the subject is to suggest that you sit down and think before you act. Look at pictures in dog books or go for a walk with dog-owning friends and observe the different moves their dogs make. More importantly, watch what the owners do and how the dog responds to them. As a mental exercise, try to spot the similarities but be careful not to comment on them. Friends will rarely accept criticism, especially from someone who doesn't know their dog as well as they think *they* do.

Striking with a paw for attention

This may be intended as a shove of rejection but it usually has totally the opposite effect!

Body language — communicating with your dog
Interpret your dog's poses and postures correctly and respond accordingly to achieve a good working relationship

1. **Your dog at play — how does he tell you that he wants to play?**
Common signals
- front paws thrust out
- raised hind quarters
- agitated behaviour and barking

Your reaction — (a) If you want to play too, mimic him
- pat your knees
- bend over
- make a grab

(b) If you don't want to play
- ignore him or tap him on the nose
- squat down (don't bend)

2. **Aggression — can you see when he is angry at you?**
Common signals
- rigid body
- ears back
- teeth bared

Situation — at the approach of strangers; when over-scolded by an owner; when food is taken from him; possessiveness to one owner in particular.

Your reaction — do not transmit the equivalent signals
- rigid body
- grimacing and pointing
- low menacing, angry voice and fixed stare

Instead —
- keep calm and avoid eye contact
- move away from open door leaving exit clear
- throw something noisy at him and feign a rush at him, then ignore him

• if the dog's exit is blocked, then try to walk away in a positive manner.

3. Submission — can you tell when he is nervous?

Common signals • tail down or tucked under
• dog keeps low to the ground
• sidles up slowly
• whimpers and rolls over to expose belly

Situation — confusion, over-correcting, over-use of physical force, lack of confidence

Your reaction — • make yourself smaller by kneeling
• talk quietly and confidently
• accept the submission by stroking his underside

4. Attention seeking — how does your dog try to attract your attention?

Common signals • paw striking on your body
• mouthing your hands

Situation — he wants to play

Your reaction — if you don't want to play
• avoid mimicking with a shove
• smack him on the head and say NO

Chapter 2
Chewing

Case histories

Name Benji **Breed** Mongrel **Sex** Male
Age 2 years

This dog suffered from the most common complaint in the Furdiths' casebook:

Distressed owner: 'Our dog is eating the house.'

Furdiths consultant: 'Is he into the walls yet?'

Distressed owner: 'Yes, and the doors, floors, and even the rubber door stopper on the washing machine.'

An appointment was made to see this monster and in due course I arrived at a modern-style estate house on the city outskirts. It was obvious they had a dog as soon as I walked through the door: the hall carpet was curled up to the kitchen door, and a waste-bin had thrown itself across the living room. The door frame of the very chic front door was missing, and had been chewed to knee level and there was also the faint but distinct aroma of doggy dung drifting on the air.

The monster turned out to be the most gorgeous, excitable bundle of hair you could imagine. All of 12 inches tall, built like a whippet with a dishmop on its head. Friendly little soul, I thought, rubbing his upturned tummy. Butter wouldn't melt in his mouth.

Brian, the owner, explained that the dog would have to go

if I couldn't help, because both partners had to work to pay the household bills.

I settled down and opened my battered case, took out my note pad and started asking questions.

'Has Benji any other problems apart from his chewing that may be bothering you?' I asked.

As it turned out he had. Although he was walked every evening when the owners came home, he was never allowed off the lead because he always ran away. As a result, Benji only messed in the garden or in the house.

'Is he O.K. at night?'

'Yes. As good as gold.'

'Where does he sleep?'

'At the top of the stairs in his basket outside our door.'

I then asked about his feeding habits. When they told me what and when he was fed the problem began to unravel itself much as I had expected it would. Benji was eating a complete dried food diet with a bit of fresh or canned meat to make it more tasty, twice a day. In addition, he was also being given chews, marrowbone biscuits and other treats to keep him going.

Moving on, I asked if Benji could be put out in the garden for a few minutes. This done, I told his owners that I would hide at the top of the stairs and once I was out of sight, they should let him in. They were then to go through the motions of leaving him to 'go to work' but instead of driving off I asked them to wait in the car and come back after five minutes. Everything was ready. Benji came in from the garden and they said their fond farewells to him as we had arranged. I waited at the top of the stairs. The door shut behind them. Benji started to pace the hall. Then he barked timidly and pawed the door. Slowly at first but then with great abandon he attacked it bodily, tearing with his mouth and claws at the doorframe, until he was in quite a frenzy. Catching one end of the carpet he started to tug at it until it rolled back. Suddenly he jumped up at the window-sill barking. Then he went back to the door and became quiet. The whole sequence had lasted no more than three minutes but the damage he had done was extensive and I was quite thankful that we had taken the precaution of putting anything he had

Chewing and destructive behaviour can be caused by many things . . .

not already chewed yet out of harm's way.

For a few seconds Benji stayed where he was. At first I was tempted to go to him, thinking a fit had taken place, but I had no time. Suddenly he was up and running again but this time his behaviour was slightly different. Tail wagging, ears erect, he was pounding the carpet in sheer ecstasy with his front paws. Then I heard it too: the key in the lock. Down to the floor went his head, bottom in the air. He wants to play, I thought. Then the figure at the door screamed like a siren possessed (her normal greeting). Barking madly Benji turned circles in the room in greeting and then just as suddenly as he had started, he stopped. Another figure had appeared at the door. Benji's tail went down, his ears went back and he began to slink away. The door opened.

'See — he knows he's done wrong,' Brian shouted and stormed toward the dog.

'Stop!' I shouted, coming down from my hiding place.

He came to a halt.

'What are you doing?' I asked.

'I'm going to teach him a lesson,' he said, looking past me at the terrified dog.

Apparently this was a regular event. If Jenny got in first, she would rant and rave and chase Benji out into the garden. Unfortunately Brian was less tolerant. He believed in taking Benji to the door, showing him the damage he had caused and beating him. I sat the pair of them down quietly and explained exactly what had gone wrong and how the problem could be dealt with.

In the first place, I pointed out Benji was being overfed on the wrong sort of food (high protein) and at the wrong times. His diet was totally unsuitable for his sedentary lifestyle. Dried food, a complete food, gives a dog all the nutrients it needs to enable it to lead a normal life. Adding the fresh meat upset the balance: it worked like rocket fuel. Secondly, he was not getting enough exercise. The garden, although large, was boring. He needed to be able to run loose in fields and wide open spaces.

The main problem was one which was self-inflicted. Benji had Jenny and Brian's attention all the time — even at night he slept only 5 feet away from them. Consequently, when they put on their hats and coats in the morning he automatically assumed that it was time for his walk. Instead, his humans said goodbye, told him that they loved him, patted him and disappeared out of the front door. Then, a big, red Ford monster swallowed them up, growled and ran away. This was all very confusing for Benji. Why were they leaving without him? He couldn't understand it so he would chew the door, to try to escape. Then he would jump up at the windows to see if they were there and then back to the door again when he found they weren't. This must have been happening several times a day while he was on his own, probably every time he heard a car go past.

But at last the relief of the homecoming. 'Someone's footsteps coming down the path. Which one is it? Mum, great! The key in the lock, the door opens and in she comes barking excitedly. She must be pleased with me!' Of course Jenny was in fact as mad as hell but as she raised her voice it became shrill as a dog's does when he or she gets very excited. That sparked off the game of run-around which

Jenny joined in, and which ended with a reward — he was let out into the garden so that he could relieve himself.

Then more footsteps. 'Who's that?, Dad! Run and hide. I hate Dad, he's never happy after work like Mum. I do my best. I show him I know he's boss but he comes and drags me from my bed and attacks me. Dominant bully.'

Hence Brian's interpretation: 'He knows he's done wrong.'

Not really. He is so used to being beaten, he fears Brian's homecoming.

'A dangerous thing', I told Brian. 'One day he will growl and snap at you.'

'He does,' said Brian, who was by now quite still and listening very intently.

'Soon Benji will read the situation and go into an attack pose first,' I said.

'Gosh.' They echoed in unison.

We started to piece together a programme of correction. The diet had to change and so did the times of the feed. Under the new system, Benji would get one feed first thing in the morning, just dried food on its own. The biscuit tin was banned. In future, exercise would consist of a walk twice a day, once in the morning before work and then again in the evening to take care of his minor problems and to calm him down. During these walks, he would, for most of the time, be kept firmly under control. No pulling, no sniffing but then, about half-way, plenty of free time in a park or a field to work off all that destructive mental and physical energy.

Sleeping was another key point which had to be sorted out. Benji had to be persuaded to sleep away from them in the kitchen. For the first few nights it would be unbearable but this would pass provided Jenny and Brian adopted the following cunning plan.

'Put him to bed, pretend to go, shut the door to the kitchen and wait. If he starts to scratch the door and throw himself up against it get hold of a small paperback book, open the door, say "No!" (do not scream) and throw the book in. Then close the door and walk away. When you have done this, you can resort to plan number two. Leave Brian's socks by the door. Benji will probably be sniffing at the base of the door to see if you are around to repeat the show. If the socks are there, your smell is there, so you are there and, unless he enjoys having books thrown at him, he'll probably go to his bed, settle down and go to sleep.' (That managed to raise a laugh as I hoped it would.) 'In the morning', I continued, 'when you go out, slam the door and start the car but don't get in and drive off straight away. Wait five minutes. If he scratches, then one of you should go to the door, open it, throw the book at him, shut the door and sneak off to work. Coming home again will be the most tense time. Open the door and *ignore* anything he has done. Taking no notice of his play, go to the back door and let him out. After five or ten minutes, bring him in as normal and greet him as warmly as you like. Because Benji's relationship with Brian has been so badly damaged, when you open the kitchen door Brian, bend down and offer him one of his favourite biscuits. Don't grovel to him though, keep your voice at its normal pitch when you are holding it out. If he hesitates, leave it on the floor, walk past him and let him follow. When he reaches you, offer your hand casually and tickle his ears. Do not overpower him or give him too much attention.'

I went over the programme with Jenny and Brian several times until all their queries had been satisfied. I arranged another appointment to see them in a fortnight's time but as usual I left my phone number at Furdiths so they could contact me if they had problems beforehand.

I heard nothing the first week. The second week I received a message on the answering machine to postpone the next visit. Three weeks later I returned a little apprehensively to the house. When I arrived, I noticed various changes; a new door frame had been fitted and the house had a fresher smell to it. Jenny looked a lot more relaxed.

'Why so happy?' I asked.

She showed me into the lounge. There on the floor with Benji, sharing his 'bed' (an old blanket) was Brian, smiling happily. Perhaps the strain has been too much!

'Has he finally flipped?' I whispered to Jenny.

Brian chuckled: 'I could never warm to him before, but look at him now, he's a different dog and so lovable.'

'Great,' I said, 'But what about the chewing?'

'He didn't go much on the book in the morning either,' said Brain.

'And the messing?' I asked.

'That's stopped too. It must have been the change in diet.'

Feeling pleased with myself I asked if there were any more problems that needed sorting out. Having drawn up an anti-chew training programme, I had then set to work on another designed to ensure that Benji would come back when he was called. To test it out, we went to the local park and let the dog off the lead. The rest was pure simplicity. (I will cover the method I used more fully in chapter 7).

I was touched by the scene in the park. A family at play, two humans and a dog acting as a unit, where before there had been only beatings, frustration, damage and despair. It was very moving to watch.

Although that case is now closed I do receive the odd update from Jenny and Brian on Benji's progress. Apparently he has never regressed. He is now six years old and has another dog and a baby to contend with but he takes it all in his stride.

Chewing and destructive behaviour can be caused by many things, not just stress as in Benji's case. Boredom is often to blame.

Name Honey **Breed** Labrador **Sex** Female **Age** 13 months

Anxious owner: Our dog chews everything and the man at the RSPCA said if they take her they will put her down. We don't want to have her put to sleep so you are our last hope. Can you help?

Furdiths consultant: 'When would you like me to come over?'

I visited Tina and John, Honey's owners, on a particularly awful day in February (I remember because it was a late visit and my shoes had been wet all day). The little girl who answered the door asked me if I was going to let her keep her dog. I nodded.

The problem was basically this: Honey was chewing everything within easy reach at night, walls, cushion flooring, even the cooker knobs.

'Does she only chew things at night?' I asked.

'Yes, mainly, but also if we're out a long time,' John said.

'What's she fed on?'

'Canned food and mixer twice daily. Oh, and a few bits and bobs.'

Then came the clincher.

'What's she like outside?'

'OK. She comes back when we call her,' Tina said.

'When you take her for a walk how much of the time does she spend on the lead?'

'None at all. We go in the car to the park every evening. She pulls on the lead you see.'

When I heard these words, I knew what I was dealing with. It appeared that the dog was getting 3 hours' exercise a day and Tina and John couldn't understand why, after a few minutes, she wanted to go again. They had made the excuse to themselves that Honey was hyperactive.

As I saw it, the problem stemmed from her slightly bad feeding habits, combined with the complete lack of mental stimulus. The dog was leading a simple life and did not have enough tasks with which to keep her brain occupied. When she was out walking, everything happened at her speed. She ran, dawdled and sniffed, and never really tired herself. When she did get to go on the lead, she pulled along in her own time with nothing to occupy her mind. What I had to do was to give her something to think about. 'Let me put it in human terms,' I said to Tina and John, 'You can walk all day in a park, feed the ducks, look at the flowers or whatever — that is pleasure. It's relaxing and not very tiring. But if Mother is coming for tea, the car is broken, you've got to get into town and get things from ten shops and get back using three buses, now that *is* tiring! When you get back, and provided you've got enough time, all you'll want to do is put your feet up, lie back and have a cup of tea. That's what we'll have to do for Honey: make her think. It sounds complicated but it isn't really and should fit quite easily into your daily routine. It'll probably do you good too!'

'Right,' said John, 'What's the plan of action then?'

'The first thing we've got to do is to change her diet,' I replied. 'We reduce her mealtimes to one feed in the morning

The little girl who answered the door asked me if I was going to let her keep her dog

and we change the brand she's fed on.'

When I proposed a variety of dog food which was cheaper than the one Honey was being fed on, Tina and John were horrified but, as I pointed out to them, the dearest is not always the best.

'Stage two involves introducing Honey to controlled exercise,' I said. 'Take her out for ten to fifteen minutes two or three times a day. Keep your normal relaxed exercise and we'll concentrate on teaching her not to pull on the lead and sniff whenever she wants to.'

As a final tip, I suggested that Tina and John should wash whatever Honey had chewed in a solution of alum and that they should give her a bone to chew on.

Explanations over, we went off to the park to put the new exercise regime into practice.

Although it was agreed that I should make a second visit two weeks later, in the event it wasn't necessary. Tina rang me the day before I was due to make my visit and asked me whether it was really worth my while. Apparently, once introduced to her new lifestyle, Honey had stopped chewing and was sleeping more regularly and both Tina and John felt that she had become much closer to them.

I agreed that in the circumstances, as long as they kept up the programme, there was no real need for me to see them again.

Tina said that they would phone me if ever Honey started to chew again. I never received that phone call.

The chewing problem

Name	Problem	Cause	Cure	End result
Benji	Displayed destructive behaviour/ howled when left alone	Wrong diet not enough exercise Lack of owner understanding	Change in diet and feeding habits Plenty of exercise morning and evening Change in owners' response to the problem	Happy dog, happy owner
Honey	Destructive chewing at night	Bad feeding habits Lack of mental stimulus	Change in diet More intensive exercise	Happy dog, happy owner

All puppies want to chew, and it is natural that you should want to give them something to chew on. But a word of warning. Think carefully about what you will give him or her to play with. A poor choice of object in these early days can have disastrous consequences later on. For example, a slipper or an old shoe would seem to be the obvious choice. But if that shoe smells of you, you could well find that if he loses it, your puppy will take to chewing anything that has your smell.

Alternatively, you could always supply him with a toy, perhaps a rubber ring or a plastic bone. Unfortunately though, if he can't find his toy, you are liable to end up facing the same problem. To the dog, the rubber-backed carpet or the baby's dolls smell just as good; I've had many a frustrated owner on the phone complaining to me that their dog just will not keep to his own toys (I wonder how many babies are as bad?).

In such cases, prevention is always better than cure: give the dog a bone (beef bone only, never lamb or chicken bones). Find a helpful butcher and ask him for a two-inch ring of bone. Then remove the marrow and the bone is ready for chewing!

As the two cases described above have shown, unwanted chewing is a problem for which there is often more than one explanation. No two cases are ever the same but armed with a bit of common sense and the information in the following check-list it's a problem that I think any caring dog-owner can solve.

What if my dog chews?

- Stand back and look objectively at the problem.

- Check his diet and avoid high protein foods. If you do not work the dog, his diet should match his routine. See your vet for further advice.

- Don't give him too many toys.

- Give him bones so that he can work out any excess energy on them.

- Make time for a proper exercise routine.

- Keep to a routine where you dictate the walking pace.

- Keep the routine varied and interesting.

- Do not smack or hit him when you see the damage. This

will only stress him more. Ignoring the behaviour will prove far more constructive than resorting to violence or shouting.

● Never allow your dog upstairs.

● Ensure the room he sleeps in is out of earshot of the front door and driveway.

● If your dog starts to chew, do not go to friends and neighbours for advice. Always seek professional help before the problem gets any worse.

Chapter 3
The aggressive dog

A dog that bites is a liability. It can land you or someone else in hospital and probably in court. It may even lead to the dog's untimely death and, if third parties are involved, it can

cost you phenomenal amounts of money.

Aggression comes in many forms and is caused by a number of different factors.

Name Humphrey Breed German Shepherd Sex Male Age 2 years

It was late afternoon when I arrived home and, as I walked through the door, Judy, my wife, greeted me with the news that she had just booked me in to see Humphrey, a dog with a nasty temper.

Apparently he was only unfriendly towards visitors although he had never actually bitten anybody. Nevertheless Judy had very wisely requested that Humphrey should be fitted with a good collar in preparation for my first visit a few days later.

When I arrived at Mr and Mrs Williams' house to keep my appointment, all seemed peaceful. There were few clues which suggested that this was anything other than a normal household. Perhaps the box on top of the gatepost containing milk and letters was a bit strange but the sign above it together with the picture of a dog which read 'Take care to shut the gate. I live here,' didn't really give cause for concern.

Oh well, I thought, it can't be that bad after all.

With hindsight, I sometimes wish I had never rung that bell! Mrs Williams, a lady of about fifty opened the door to me and I went into a long Victorian hallway. At the end of the hall there was a door and the fearsome growls and scrabblings I heard coming from behind it told me that Humphrey was not far away.

Suddenly the door opened and I was face to face with him a scrabbling ball of fury with saliva dribbling from his jowls.

'Oh my god,' I thought, 'It's a maniac.'

As he hit the carpet I knew somehow he was going to bite. I looked to his mistress for support, only to find her sliding majestically down the wall in a deep faint. I was on my own. Humphrey charged me, leapt at me and bumped into my briefcase. As he did I noticed he was wearing his collar and silently thanking Judy for saving my life, I grabbed him in a style I had learned from Tarzan and held on with both hands like a shipwrecked sailor. Sweating, cursing, and struggling I managed to straddle him and steered him back towards his cell, no mean feat given that he weighed about 120 lbs and seemed to be about ten feet tall. By this time, Mr Williams, the unsuspecting instigator of the drama (it was he who had opened the kitchen door) and its only survivor had arrived on the scene and was chanting 'Good boy, steady, good boy,' from the sidelines.

'Shut up', I screamed. 'You're making things worse.'

He stopped in mid flow and went very quiet and I turned my attention to getting grumpy old Humphrey back into his cell. Once he was in, I slammed the door shut holding the knob tightly whilst Mr Williams stirred himself and slid a small bolt across. Safe for a while at least!

'Now, let's see to your wife,' I volunteered.

'She's okay. It always happens when the dog attacks,' he mumbled.

I helped Mrs Williams back on to her feet and we adjourned to the lounge to sort things out.

'Well,' I said, 'I am annoyed to say the least. You said he didn't bite.'

'I'm sorry, but we thought you wouldn't come if we said how bad he was,' Mrs Williams replied.

This excuse sounded familiar. It happens quite regularly. I suppose it is hard to imagine that someone can rebuild something from a situation to which there seems to be only one solution.

It transpired that Humphrey had been behaving like this since the age of 1. He had already bitten the milkman and a meter reader and as a result of this second incident, Mr and Mrs Williams had received a warning from the police to control their dog or he would have to be put down. They took him out for walks, but only late at night in order to avoid other dogs. However he caused no problems when they let him off his lead and once I knew this, the rest was easy.

'You are the cause of the trouble, I'm afraid,' I told them.

'In what way?' Mr Williams asked.

'Well, quite simply you have, through your actions, trained your dog to attack. Quiet unintentionally, I'm sure.'

'But we don't let him do it. We shout "No" at him, and I've

tried hitting him on the bottom but he gets worse!' Mrs Williams exclaimed.

'Yes. He will. When you go to the door or someone arrives you grab him by the collar, yes?'

'Yes, so that he doesn't jump all over them.'

'Quite. When you see someone coming do you wrap his lead around your hands or pull him into your side?'

'Yes.'

'Well then it looks to me as if you are the cause of your own problem.'

I explained to them that by tensing up and trying to hold the dog back they were suggesting to him that they were apprehensive of the visitor or passer-by. Humphrey therefore adopted a protective role to keep them from being harmed.

During the attacks Humphrey interpreted his owner's shouts as barks of encouragement from his 'pack' and was similarly encouraged when they tried to calm him down afterwards. But, and this was the key, he never prepared for attack when he was off the lead. In this situation there was no stimulus coming from them, he was 'off duty', if you like. Either that or he lacked the confidence to act on his own.

The road to recovery for Humphrey would not be long, but tedious, I explained to them.

'How long will it take?' asked Mr Williams.

'About three weeks,' I replied, adding that I would probably only need to arrange one or two more visits.

'That quickly. We expected you to say six months like the other chap,' he said.

'What other chap?' I asked.

Apparently I had not been the first to try to cure Humphrey of his problem.

Mr Williams explained that an ex-police dog handler from the local obedience club had also had a go. He had decided that Humphrey was a 'top dog' who needed a sound beating because that is what dogs understand. He had used a phrase I hate: 'You have to be cruel to be kind'.

Mr Williams went on, 'He came every week and took Humphrey out for a walk with a muzzle on him.'

'Did you go along?' I asked.

'I did, to start with,' said Mr Williams, but I don't like seeing animals suffer and he used to make Humphrey scream.'

'What did he do?'

'He asked me to hold him and then he put a chain on him. After that, he came up to me and touched me — if Humph growled I had to let go of the lead. He then tugged him away on his lead and chain and kicked him over and over until he stopped.'

'Why did you stop the treatment?' I asked.

'Humphrey didn't like him, and we couldn't get a muzzle on him after the second time,' said Mrs Williams.

'Humphrey would hide under the table when he came in and growl at him. He said that Humphrey was mad and would have to be put down.'

Mr and Mrs Williams had obviously had a very bad experience at the hands of this so-called 'handler' and as I was at pains to persuade them, he was in no way representative of dog-trainers in general.

It is worth remembering when you are faced with a severe problem, that, by and large, clubs tend to be run by amateurs. As long as they perform a function as social clubs, and provided you can find one that doesn't insist on choke (or check) chains then they can do little harm and they can be beneficial in promoting a common bond among dog owners. Do choose carefully though. Even if the instructor is an ex-dog handler it doesn't necessarily mean that he has the relevant experience to cope effectively with the problem.

A dog handler working for the police, the prison services or even a private security firm merely handles a piece of machinery that has been trained for him. He knows what words to use to make it work, nothing more. Given that a dog's working life spans approximately ten years, your average handler will probably have had experience of working with only one dog in his career and although responsible for the dog's upkeep, he will not have been responsible for training it. His counterpart in the civilian world is normally someone whose only qualification is that they have trained their own dog and want to go further. So you have to be very careful about whom you go to. Cruelty, even if it is unintentional, must be prevented at all costs — I heartily disapprove of choke chains and detest people who are 'cruel to be kind'.

Having reassured them that my approach to dealing with Humphrey's problem would be totally different from that adopted by our dog-handler friend, I asked them to put him on a lead and meet me outside.

I went outside and prepared myself for my second meeting with Humphrey. A few minutes later the door opened and out they came, Humphrey in front dragging Mrs Williams behind him. Humphrey caught sight of me and ploughed over to have a closer look.

'Hold him back,' I called, starting to walk backwards around the car.

'I am,' she said.

'Let him go,' I said.

They couldn't hold him any longer anyway. As he came forward, I grabbed the lead and ran, dragging a very befuddled Humphrey with me. As I turned towards the equally befuddled owners again Humphrey had stopped jumping at my arm and was quietly observing me at lead's length.

'Right,' I panted, 'Now we will see what we can do. You're probably wondering why Humphrey didn't make much of an attempt to savage me this time.'

Mr and Mrs Williams both nodded.

'Well, there wasn't really any fun in it for him, nobody praised him. What's more I had bare arms.'

Mr and Mrs Williams were somewhat puzzled at this but as I explained to them, it's my own well-established theory that clothes, together with the excited screaming and jumping of the victim, are the things that trigger the aggression. If you can keep calm and ignore your attacker it will really upset him because it's not a game any more.

I showed them my method of making a dog walk to heel and behave (the 'instant miracle' to be described more fully on page 70).

I gave Humph back to Mrs Williams after and showed her exactly how to hold the lead and use it. We then set off around the block, I went through the details coaching gently:

'Do not let him cock his leg. Give him a "no" and pull him away as you have been shown.'

To explain this treatment is very easy and there is a good

reason for applying it: if you can dictate where your dog leaves his mark, he will respect you all the more. You are in control.

Once shown the way it took about two minutes for Humph to click into walking quietly.

Then we met a dog.

'When his ears prick up, correct him with a "no" and pull him as before,' I whispered. 'Remember, don't shout.'

Humphrey's ears started to flinch, and she caught him well. She stumbled a little but managed to walk on once more and he ignored the other dog, a snarling yapping Westie that was dragging its owner home for tea. We arrived home without further mishap and then I set about dealing with the indoor problem.

I knew that the owners could never hold Humph on a long lead (Mr Williams had a stick) so I decided to be devious. The plan was quite simple. We attached the end of his long lead to the banisters of the stairs and to the other end I attached a clip. When visitors were expected, Humphrey was put on his line and left. There was enough slack to enable him to move about the kitchen and his bed, but not quite enough to let him reach the front door. When the visitors knocked at the door, the Williams let Humph head for it and then when he was almost there whoever was the nearest said 'no' sharply but not loudly. Because of his speed, Humphrey would execute a complete backflip when he hit the end of the line. The owner could ignore him completely, go to the front door and open it. The result that first time was fantastic. I shall always remember it, the look of bewildered amazement on that dog's face as he stopped and watched while Mrs Williams opened the door to the next door neighbour. As Humph looked at him, he tossed a ball (Humph's favourite) down the hall. Humph ran, picked it up and stood there looking bewildered as the door shut.

'That's it for this week,' I said.

'But we can't keep him on the long lead forever,' Mrs Williams said with obvious alarm.

'We won't,' I promised. 'Next week we'll start to let him off it.'

The following week I arrived full of concern. I had heard

nothing all week. (I had expected at least one phone call.)

'Oh well,' I thought. 'No news is good news.' I rang the bell, picking up a football in readiness.

The door opened. Humph leapt towards me and stopped. I threw the ball and held my breath. He ran and picked it up and to my delight brought it back (although still growling) to the front door.

'No,' said Mr Williams and invited me in. Humph looked at me for a few minutes and dropped his ball, wagging his tail. Ignoring him, we went to the lounge for a progress report. Mrs Williams told me she could 'cope' outside but found it a little difficult. Humph did not lunge at dogs any more but he did pull towards them. This was disappointing. 'And how is he indoors?' I asked.

'Quite good, he stops before he reaches the door now, and seems to enjoy the ball game, but he's still on the line, isn't he?'

'Not for long,' I said and launched into phase two of my plan.

During the second week we disconnected the line from the banisters so that he could drag it with him, but everyone carried on as before, pretending that he was still tied up.

We went on to discuss the rest of my master plan. Once released from his banister Humphrey would be allowed to sleep with his ball. This I hoped would encourage him to bring it to the door expecting a game. We shortened the line every day by about three to four feet, so that each time he would feel less drag on his collar until finally he would forget it altogether. I also suggested that when he went out for his walks he was fitted with a head collar. This is a new concept but quite humane, and once he can be controlled and when he is used to it, the dog will stop the pulling.

That week, the Williamses did call me to tell me how damned difficult the head collar was to put on Humphrey because he thought it was a muzzle. He was wearing it but he was not happy. I suggested that he should wear it at feed times as well as when walking, to see what would happen. Fortunately they phoned again at the end of the week to say he now looked a lot happier and, yes, I was right: he didn't pull.

When the fortnight was up I went back to see Humphrey.

Not quite an olive branch, perhaps, but just as gratefully accepted

I was again apprehensive because he was completely loose: I rang the bell and, remembering my first visit, I felt quite vulnerable. Mrs Williams appeared and flung the door wide open (nothing like going for broke I thought), then Humphrey appeared at the kitchen door, disappeared and then reappeared a moment later with something in his mouth. It was one of Mrs Williams' best cushions he had bundled up like a year-old fool of a dog. Snorting and wagging his tail he placed his gift in my hand and actually let go, better than I had even dreamed! I could think of nothing to do but return his gesture, so without further ado I took off my shoe and gave it to him. I don't know why, but it seemed appropriate.

I later retrieved my shoe and have never felt inclined to go that far again. I took Humphrey's gesture with the cushion as a token of peace, not quite an olive branch, perhaps but just as gratefully accepted.

For our second aggression case I have selected something from the other end of the scale. What I would term a dominance aggression or the 'top dog' syndrome. Humphrey did not suffer from this syndrome but there are certain similarities.

Superdog!

Name Dan **Breed** Mini Schnauzer **Sex** Male Age 18 months

Referred by letter:

Our problem is driving us mad. Dan has started biting us at odd times. We cannot walk him and my husband wants him put down. Dan has been away for training, and it was super to see him jumping over jumps at the kennels but although the trainer said he was cured, as soon as we got him home he was up to his old tricks again.

We really do feel that we cannot go on but I cannot bear to think of him being put to sleep before we have tried everything. Please get in touch if there is anything you can do. You really are our last hope.

I receive many letters like this one, always with that last line: 'You are our last resort.'

I phoned Mrs Page in due course and advised her that I might be able to help but would have to see the dog personally.

I could hear Dan barking as soon as I rang the bell. He was a nice-looking little animal and I developed quite a soft spot for him. His owners were a very pleasant couple. Quiet, gentle and totally doting on their Danny Boy. That was their mistake.

'Have a seat and we'll tell you all about him,' Mr Page invited.

I sat and listened to a tale so familiar that I was tempted to take it up from them before they had finished telling it to me.

'We got Dan from a rescue centre. He was six months old and very skinny. The people said he had belonged to a family that had no time for him, and rather than have him put down they gave him to the centre. We are his third home and we do not think he could possibly go back. The man we spoke to said if they took Dan back he would be destroyed because he was nasty.'

'What exactly is the problem?' I enquired.

'He has become very grumpy over the last few months,' said Mrs Page.

'Be honest, dear, he's been like it more or less since we got him. It's just got worse,' said Mr Page.

'When is he grumpy?'

'If we have a cuddle he growls and comes between us. If we try to make him do something he doesn't want to he growls and shows his teeth, and if he's on a chair we just can't move him.'

'What is he like about food?'

'Terrible. He brings things in or steals them and then guards them. That's when he bit John.'

John had a lovely set of scars across his hands and he still had a bandage on his arm.

'I tried to take some tissues away from him,' John explained.

'Fine. What is his general behaviour like outside?'

'He pulls,' Mrs Page replied.

'And barks,' added John.

'Barks?' I queried.

'Yes as he goes out of the door he sets up a heck of a noise, yapping and barking, he just won't stop.'

'Where does he sleep?' I asked.

'On our bed. He always has done.'

'Well,' I said, 'It's quite simple. You have a dominance problem. Dan thinks of you as his pack and because of the way you treat him, he believes he is the leader of that pack.'

'But we thought that because he had been treated so badly he needed love.'

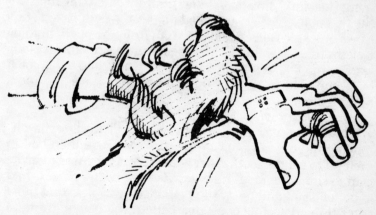

John had a lovely set of scars across his hands

'He does,' I said, 'But in the right way.'

Because his owners wanted to compensate for his past they were over-kind and reasoning, and treated the problem as one would treat a disturbed human. The dog had misread their intentions. He had in these two humans, a pair of eager followers. When he growled, they cowered, they crouched down, extended their hands, and talking in a soothing way. This is very similar to the way a weaker dog will submit to a more powerful one. He was allowed to sleep on the bed, a place reserved for the leaders. Sometimes there was a minor power play; they would take things from him (or try). When he snapped, they quite sensibly backed off. In fact in adopting this approach they had effectively made a rod for their own backs.

The barking was a classic act of leadership. Dan was warning strangers off his patch and calling the pack to follow him, in this case the humans who lived with him. My first task was to reassure them that the problem could be corrected.

As usual, I explained that only they could cure it, but that I would guide them through the steps they needed to take. It would be tough going and for the next few weeks their own behaviour would need to be very positive. There would be no room for 'It's raining so I won't do it tonight.'

To start with we broke the problem into various departments for simplicity. Taking the stress out of feeding time was the first objective. It was agreed that Dan would be fed at set times only. Mr Page would feed him from the bowl, holding it all the time. Meanwhile Mrs Page would keep him on a long lead (a thin line, ten to fifteen feet long) attached to his collar by a clip. The plan was that she should leave the room holding the other end.

If the dog growled, Mr Page had to say 'no.'

When Mrs Page heard this, she was to pull the line sharply, moving the dog away from the dish, Mr Page then had to pretend to eat the food. After a few seconds he was to invite Dan to share the food. If he growled again, the process had to be repeated and he was to be pulled away a second time. After three days following this pattern the owners were to swap roles.

Second on the agenda were Dan's sleeping habits. His days of sleeping upstairs had ended. It was the kitchen or nothing for our little friend. 'Ignore the noise and warn the neighbours,' I said. 'You mustn't disturb him until the morning. If you have to go back into the kitchen for some reason, do it when he is quiet.'

'Why?' asked Mr Page.

'Because if you go back when he's noisy he'll win the game,' I said.

Dan's reaction to his owners' cuddles and body contact was a slightly different kettle of fish. I took the liberty of explaining that I believed Dan thought this was an encroachment on his bitch (Mrs Page) by an opposing male (Mr Page). He was simply protecting his interests by driving them apart. Treatment was simple; our friend the paperback book was the ideal solution.

When they cuddled they should each try to have a paperback book concealed in their hands. When Dan growled at them they had to say 'no' and throw the book at him, then ignore him and carry on cuddling. If he started again they had to repeat the process.

'It really is that simple,' I told them, 'but be careful never to

Dan thought this was an encroachment on his bitch

threaten him with your book. Never raise it in anger or wave it at him, or you will only antagonize him. The book only works because it is fast and blends with its surroundings. Following a throw, act normally. After a few minutes, if you are walking past him, give him a quick "Hello", and a pat as if nothing had happened.'

'What about the things he steals?' asked Mrs Page. 'The tissues and towels and things.'

'Book him! Say "no" and throw the book. When he backs off in surprise, pick up the object casually and walk off with it.'

'And what about walking? I can't stand the barking, it's so embarrassing.'

This was simplicity itself. I fitted him with a collar (*not* a choke chain) and lead. As Mr Page opened the door, he said 'no' and pulled him sideways away from the door. Once outside we used the sideways pull with 'heel' or 'no.' In this way we taught him to walk properly.

To use a choke chain pulling the dog backwards on it — a method favoured by dog clubs — relies on the dog hearing the chain click, then reacting to the backwards pull. I believe this is an ineffective method of controlling your dog, mainly because it teaches the animal to respond to a noise and then pain so that once off the chain you have lost your means of control.

The other method, which amateurs usually resort to, is to let the dog run forward on its long training lead and chain and then to pull back hard inflicting maximum pain to 'teach him a lesson!'

Simultaneously they scream 'heel' or 'leave.' If you adopt this plan of action you either succeed in gaining control of a dog that fears you or, as is more often the case, the dog will attack you because he has heard the chain coming. Of course you may get away with it if you're lucky but take note of the experience of the person who sent me this letter saying:

I am having problems with Shep he has become very aggressive, he bit me the other night when I was about to take the chain off the door!

He doesn't appear to like the choke chain, as soon as I try to put it on him he dives under the table and looks quite wild, and growls as I try to put it on.

Their dog went as far as to attack them and to urinate when it heard the door chain rattle!

The Furdiths' method works on a different principle. The collar is fitted at all times. It should be flat, not rounded, comfortable and non-restrictive. Attaching the lead to this (always a rope lead, never a chain) we immediately take away the noise factor, and the rabbit-in-a-snare element which occurs when the dog feels a chain constricting it, pulls to escape and succeeds only in creating yet more pressure as the chain gets tighter still.

Instead of pulling backwards and grappling, the owner pulls sideways, parallel with the dog's neck and keeps walking. Never praise the dog or change the tone of your voice but adopt an 'I didn't do it' look and walk on regardless. Keep your voice at its normal pitch; never shout or become excited.

To sum up:

● Pull sideways instead of back. This is easier for you. It also duplicates a natural correction method used by other dogs: a simple nip on the neck and a growl (only humans moan and whinge).

● Don't praise. Dogs don't do it and it can be very confusing to your dog. Either he will behave well because he is expecting a reward or he will interpret your praise as a form of cowering to him. You correct him and then you apologize. How contradictory can you get? Correcting and continuing as normal is far and away the best approach to the problem.

● Control the level and tone of your voice. In home environments a dog will be expected to respond to the orders of three or four people. If someone slaps their thighs like a panto act, Dad shouts, and Mum soothes, the dog is likely to end up being thoroughly confused. So use your normal voice, and get everybody else in the family to do the same. If you don't raise your voice from the start, you will probably never have to. There is nothing more annoying than a bellower.

Speak to the dog as though you have a hangover — that way,

it will never matter if you have! This is the 'Instant Miracle' cure.

Mr and Mrs Page soon picked up the 'Instant Miracle method.' We employed a 'no' and a light pull followed by a 'heel' every time Dan cocked his leg. After a run in the park and a controlled walk back, we arrived home.

'You must go in first,' I said.

Once in the living room I wrote a programme for Dan who was by this time gently snoring in a corner, totally worn out after all his exertions.

'Right. Any questions before I disappear?'

'Why do we have to go in and out before the dog does?' asked Mr Page.

'Easy. You have spent 30 minutes or so showing him who's boss. It is the leader's privilege to go in and out first. In — to grab the best bed, girl, or food before the rabble, out — to warn off the bad guys. If you let him go in while you hang back to take your wellies off he might see this as a last minute backdown and then all the hard work you have put in with him during the walk will have been for nothing.'

Although he spent three days sulking, Dan eventually accepted everything quite willingly and soon became quite set in his new pattern. As far as I know, he has never reverted to his bad old self but that is the beauty of the plan. Once taught the new routine, the owners understand it and as a result their animals understand it too.

Humphrey and Dan illustrate two common problems.

Humphrey's owners simply took on a dog that was too big and too boisterous for them. They did not give due consideration to their age and general fitness when they chose him and once the problems started, they were confused. In Dan's case his owners hadn't fully researched their subject before they took the plunge.

Learning about the normal behaviour of dogs in their natural, free state can be extremely useful.

The dog is a pack animal — a well worn cliché and one all dog owners are familiar with. Most people believe a pack is the equivalent of a human family. It isn't. In a pack, the animal lives within a structure and follows certain rules which bear no relation whatsoever to ours. Where we reason, dogs do not, where we explain, dogs snap. Where we let our arguments rage on for days and days, dogs forget immediately.

In a dog pack, there is one leader. If he gives an order he follows it up physically — not with rolled-up newspapers but with a sharp snap or nip. It is a very disciplined existence, in which the strongest will lead and challenges are many. To keep his position, the male has to be dominating. The dog owner must therefore find a way to cope with this dominance.

Mental instability

Aggression caused by mental illness is the only side of my job that genuinely frightens me and as yet I haven't found a way to beat it.

Of course there are always going to be a percentage of dogs that suffer mental illness of one kind or another from birth, but the type of instability which I am referring to here is man-made, the result of interbreeding caused either by the quest for a perfect animal or by a greed to meet the demands of fashion.

Some breeds suffer more than others, although I believe that what is termed 'rage syndrome' in Cocker Spaniels is a complaint affecting most pedigree breeds in one form or another.

For instance the tale of the Dobermann who is given to attacking its owners for no apparent reason is one which I've heard many times. And why does the German Shepherd have such a reputation for aggressiveness? Is it because of this reputation that it is so frequently cast as a guard dog? Why do Retrievers of both sexes show sudden aggression to their owners and remain calm in between? I could go on but I think that at this point a brief case history would be of more use, demonstrating as it does just how devastating the effect of interbreeding can be. Obviously the name of the owners has been changed, but I have been given permission to retain the dog's true breed and name for accuracy and as a warning to others.

Name Ben Breed Dalmatian Age 2 years

This family had adopted a sensible and responsible attitude to the duties involved in caring for a dog and they had no reason to suspect that he would cause them any problems. Ben was a seemingly healthy 2 year-old Dalmatian who had been in the family from the age of 6 weeks. My first impression of Ben was that he seemed to be a friendly dog with a well-balanced attitude to humans. I listened to his owners explain that when their daughter Susan arrived home from school, Ben greeted her but then started to growl. However, if Susan left him alone, within minutes he returned to normal. He would also growl savagely at her in the evenings. Susan was a sensible 17-year-old girl and had been living at home since the day Ben arrived.

The problem had started a year earlier on the day that Ben returned from a short stay in kennels. Significantly though it had always been Susan who was singled out for the special treatment. Armed with this knowledge I diagnosed the problem as a sexual one and set about trying to cure it. I concentrated on reducing his ardour while at the same time encouraging Sue to show him that she was boss. It was, I hoped, going to be a simple case.

I was mistaken, as a second visit showed. Although Ben proved more easy to control outside now, Susan insisted that she was still having the same problem.

We looked at the situation again. It was strange. In general Ben was extremely friendly. He liked having his tummy rubbed by Sue which meant that he had to adopt a totally submissive posture but he didn't seem to object; Sue said she did it all the time.

I was perplexed. I even posed the problem to colleagues as a brain teaser but to no avail. I was beginning to feel sure that the case was exaggerated, and it wasn't until a further visit that I was finally convinced of what was happening.

Term time had arrived and Sue was back at school. I arrived at 6.30 pm and after discussing the problem in great depth with the family I explained that I suspected the problem to be either very deep seated or genetic. During the course of this second visit the problem manifested itself again.

Sue walked across the kitchen to make a cup of tea for everyone and Ben started to growl from his corner. It was a very low growl at first, until Sue began to return to her seat, then it rapidly turned into a deep, full growl and Ben stood up. He moved a few paces forward and then stood still, trembling from head to toe. At first I thought he was going to have a fit but he had obviously singled Sue out and was intent on directing all his attentions to her.

I put myself tactically between them and was determined to see it through to the end (normally Sue would leave the room at this point). Ben's tail was moving in a submissive mode, almost apologetically, but his body had gone completely rigid as if he had been seized by some form of muscular contraction. His head was forward, his eyes were very bloodshot and starting, his lips were curled and he was making a very loud, deep growl like a rush of wind.

I tried to distract him, first using a loud rape alarm then by holding my hand to his face and even putting it halfway into his mouth; no response. Finally I tried to distract him physically by striking him on the head but none of this had any effect on him whatsoever. If Sue tried to touch him his aggression escalated, yet I could touch him anywhere.

Then without warning Ben whimpered once and became his normal self. Once more within a minute or two he was asking Sue to rub his belly again. On two occasions that evening he reacted in the same way and I had no doubt that had I encouraged Sue to touch him she would have been very seriously injured.

The outcome was inevitable. I advised Ben's owners that for Susan's safety, the situation could not be allowed to continue. After consultations with the veterinary surgeon who was dealing with the case, Ben's life was terminated by Veterinary Euthanasia.

The family were devastated. Despite assurances to the contrary they blamed themselves and still cannot face owning another dog. However it is my belief that the cause of these tragic circumstances lay not with them but was connected with Ben's pedigree. It transpires that he was bred by a family with no knowledge of dogs who, it seems, wanted to make a quick profit from a spot of puppy selling. Ben was the product of incestuous mating. His parents were brother and sister and his grandparents were bred father to daughter. As a result, there was really very little chance that Ben would ever have led a normal well-balanced life.

Ben's case is not unique but one of several I have come up against during the past few years. In each case, the message is the same: never purchase from an unlicensed breeder.

The aggression problem

Name	Problem	Cause	Cure	End result
Humphrey	Aggressive and protective	Dog trained into role by owners who read situation incorrectly	Positive approach adopted by owners and dog reschooled into different attitude	Happy dog, happy owner
Dan	Aggression to owners – possibly sexually oriented	Soft owners who allowed him to sleep in their bedroom. Sexually dominant, owners afraid	Set feeding times. Removed from bedroom. Strong challenge to aggression using book method.	Happy dog, happy owner
Ben	Spontaneous aggression to owners' daughter	Dog interbred and unstable	None — dog destroyed	—

Correcting aggression

To be avoided

- **Rolled up newspapers** Probably the most widely used items in the 'new dog owner' collection of 'musts'. I have seen a lot of injuries caused as a direct result of using this little gem, often of both a physical (to the dog and owner) and mental (to the dog) nature.

  How? Well it's simple. When the dog is naughty, you the owner, pick up your club — the newspaper — and threaten him with it. If he persists in his behaviour, you hit him with it. Initially it instils fear into the poor devil. How many times have you heard people boasting about this?

'I only have to pick up the paper to get him to cower or go to his bed.'

But it is much more likely that sooner or later, the dog will begin to fear this object and urinate or growl when he is shown it. In such cases he is still being controlled but there is no respect involved. Alternatively, as he gets bigger, he may take the 'Is that all you can do?' attitude and meet violence with violence.

For me, respect is a very important part of any relationship; without it there is no trust. I pride myself that my own dogs are well controlled but they certainly never have cause to fear me.

- **Picking him up by the scruff of the neck and shaking him** Great! Nature's way! But only until the pup is about 6 weeks old. Dogs wean at 6–8 weeks and even Mum doesn't lift them after this time. She nips them or snaps them back into line instead. If you want to lift your dog by the neck, be warned — he could bite! Jack Russell owners might get away with it but steer clear if you've got a Rottweiler — you might never recover from the effort!

- **Grabbing him by the cheeks, looking into his eyes and shaking him** The mere thought of this makes me shudder. If you hold any dog by the cheeks (or the ears) and shake it you inflict pain. The dog's immediate reaction is to try to escape but it can't do this because you have a hold of it. This leaves your pet with only one option; he must attack his attacker! If he makes a lunge you are then in a very dangerous situation. Because of the way you are holding him, when the dog bites, your inner arms will be exposed to his teeth. If you withdraw you will only make matters worse because in his eyes this is tantamount to admitting defeat. He will remember this next time you try to correct him and he will growl immediately.

- **Shouting at him in your sternest voice** This I have always detested — it's funny isn't it the way loudness is often associated with control? When I see people shouting at their dogs to try and control them I am reminded of an old training film I once saw. This film was made in the days before videos. The dubbing was terrible. Everybody was shouting at the top of their voices in true military style, with about as much compassion as a sergeant major on a parade square. You had to praise the dog with a: 'Good boy, Fang, good boy!!'

To emphasize the point, the actor rapped Fang on the head and very nearly brain-damaged him!

There's really no need for this at all. Instead why don't you try training your dog the Standen way? It's always best to start off quietly, in a relaxed frame of mind. Remember if you are loud and jolly from the beginning you'll have to carry on like that for the duration. In mid-January, when it's sleeting or snowing and water is trickling down the back of your neck and your fingers are turning blue, will you feel like being constantly cheerful for an hour or more? What's more if you are bellowing when the dog is right under your nose, how much voice will you have left when he is 200 metres away? I would even dispute the need for voice tones when training, a point I put to the test recently when training dogs for deaf clients. For a deaf person, voice tone is virtually impossible to achieve, but as long as they carry out the dog's initial training themselves, it should respond just as well to their voice, as it would to that of a person who can hear.

Finally, spare a thought for the neighbours. Would *you* want to be woken up at six o'clock in the morning by a command of 'sit' which measured ten on the Richter scale?

- **Getting him to adopt a submissive position** What a joy to get a dog to behave submissively but how do you achieve this? Have you ever noticed that in most articles this method is included but never explained. Probably because it is often considered as the end result of a battle with an aggressive animal. It is a very sensible idea to try to get your dog to be submissive but very difficult to achieve by conventional dog training methods. Remember that your dog could be biting you at the time and if you force him into such a position he may react violently. If you use food to tempt him, he might soon come to regard this as a circus trick and you will therefore achieve very little. If you soothe and coax him, he may interpret this as an act of submission on your part and you could therefore be contributing to his dominance over you.

It would be better if this submissive position was a natural reaction adopted by a dog that genuinely respected its owner. I would advise against attempting it as a direct method.

I have been deliberately critical in the appraisal of these methods to show that a little knowledge is really quite dangerous. No doubt these methods have worked for their inventors, much as my methods have worked for me. The problems start occurring with the 'Chinese whispers effect'. People hear of these methods second and third hand and it is that which leads to their downfall.

For example, I have had people in the past who have blamed me for their dog's weight loss.

'You saw my friend's dog and you said it was being overfed on the wrong food, so we tried feeding our dog the diet you gave them. Now he's half the size he was.'

What they omitted to tell me was that their pet was a rather large wolfhound with a huge appetite whilst their friend's dog was a terrier.

My advice to you is therefore to consult an expert before you try anything. Your vet will put you in touch.

Aggression — a summary	
Avoiding aggression	• adopt a positive approach to training from day one
	• socialize your dog early, especially with regular visitors — let the postman give him a stroke

- don't take your dog to the door as a guard; leave him loose instead and let people stroke him

Controlling aggression to others

- consider the possible causes of the aggression — in many cases you may be the catalyst
- physical correction is needed but don't beat him or use newspapers, a firm smack on the head will do
- muzzle him and let the victim take him for a walk

Controlling aggression towards you

- remove the dog from the bedroom (if guilty)
- stop him from leg cocking when on a lead, pulling him away with a firm NO
- concentrate on control training, especially 'heel and come'
- muzzle your dog and use your fingers to groom him
- be forceful — never try to reason with him

Controlling nervous aggression

- when correcting him, be firm and positive

- never force your dog to accept people. Let him approach them in his own time. Tell your visitor to ignore the dog and to avoid making any sudden movements

Chapter 4

House-training

House-training problems take many forms but usually occur as a result of poor early training, the coming of age, or because of some error in the dog's exercise routine. Occasionally, veterinary reasons can explain the problem but these will be quickly identified and cleared up by your veterinary surgeon. There are no hard and fast rules when it comes to house-training your dog but one thing is sure, you will need a great deal of patience!

Harshness has never achieved anything. The parents among you should relate to this. Think of your children. If you rubbed your baby's nose in its mess there is every chance that you would either be arrested, or deprived of your child. In my opinion, if you subject your dog to this degradation, you should suffer the same punishment. Hitting the dog or 'rubbing his nose in it' is a disgusting, unsanitary habit that can cause stress to the animal and make it nervous. I find it hard to sympathize with owners who treat their dogs like this.

Let us start with the prevention of house-training problems. Your vet will probably insist that you keep the dog confined to the house for the first few weeks after you have got it and before it has been vaccinated. I would therefore recommend that you arrange to take your puppy home with you when he is about 15 weeks old. Of course this does have some disadvantages but in the long run, it will save you a lot of trouble. Invariably such dogs are steadier and easier to cope with. If you cannot wait for your new companion and want to take him home immediately, I recommend that you try to avoid puting newspapers down on the floor, except in the case of emergencies. This is because if you do put paper down, this will probably encourage you to be less vigilant. For example you may be inclined to finish your coffee before you take little Rover out into the garden but by this time it will probably be too late.

The first thing you should remember is to avoid scolding your dog if it wets on arrival at its new home. Think instead of how you would feel if half blind you had been deprived of Mum and the family and pushed into a box with an old jumper by a load of gibbering foreigners who kept poking and prodding you . . . Wouldn't you wet yourself? Remember that at this age, your puppy is very receptive to new things and learns very quickly. If you shout at him or hit him, you could be asking for trouble later on.

I find that a box of peat makes a good dog toilet. Put this near the puppy's sleeping area or near the door. When you arrive home with him put him in it. So that if he does have an accident, it will be where you want it to be. When he is elsewhere in the house watch him constantly and if you see the signs, pick him up and take him to the tray. Keep calm and don't resort to a ridiculous 'good boy' voice. The smell of the tray will be enough to trigger his responses.

Outside, prepare a patch of garden — it should be a corner that you would prefer him to use when he can go outside — for himself and empty your peat tray there every day, leaving some dry peat at one end. (If you only have a small yard, a growbag is a good substitute.) You should freshen the tray with the peat from the dry end and empty the soiled peat into a pile at the opposite end. When you come downstairs in the morning, if you find any puddles and patches, step over them, open the back door and put the offender out. Only scream when the door is firmly shut behind him! Remember, accidents are common at this stage so try to behave normally. If you behave like an ogre and start stomping about you will frighten him. To show your anger will confuse him; he will not be aware that he has done anything wrong. All he will understand is that just as he was getting ready to show you how happy he was to see you, you lashed out. Try to get your relationship with him off to a good start. In later years, a dog who has been constantly scolded in the morning by its owner, will probably be too scared to leave its bed to greet him or her.

When he starts walking properly, let him out into your garden or yard. Hopefully, in the course of his adventures, he will find the peat box which you should have placed in a strategic position outside; he may even come across the patch of garden where you clean out his tray. When he finds that his peat box is no longer available, he will soon realize that if he wants to relieve himself, he'll have to go outside and preferably in the same spot each time. It won't be roses all the way of course but if you are vigilant, can work to create a steady routine and can learn to spot the signs of forthcoming eruptions, things will gradually get better and the problem should eventually disappear altogether. Our first house-training case is one of poor early training and, one that many of you will probably be able to relate to quite well.

Name Sheeba Breed Black Labrador Sex Female Age 12 months

Mr and Mrs Lane contacted me to see if I could do anything about her dog which messed indoors *after* it had been out for long walks. I made an appointment to visit and when the time came, I went round to meet them. Sheeba was very bouncy and clumsy as Labradors tend to be but there was no outward sign of any abnormality.

'What's the problem?' I asked, 'She looks alright to me.'

'She likes to spite us, I'm afraid,' said Mrs Lane. 'We give her all the love we can, the best food, a lovely bed, but she throws it back in our face by messing indoors deliberately'

I was sure that Sheeba was not acting out of spite but I forced a diplomatic reply and they continued to tell me how they had 'tried everything to make her see sense.'

I decided that it was probably the owners who needed the help but I had to ask them a number of questions before I could offer them the right advice.

We started with Sheeba's basic diet — fresh food from the

butcher's in the evening, toast for breakfast and biscuits at lunch-time.

'Is she overfed?' they asked me.

Again I answered as diplomatically as possible and then moved on quickly to the matter of exercise.

'Well, that's the part we resent most. She has two long walks per day and she has the garden to play in.'

I have to admit that their reply somewhat baffled me. She appeared to be getting plenty of exercise, so a lack of exercise was obviously not the cause of the problem.

'What's she like outside?' I asked.

'No worse than any other dog,' said Mr Lane.

'She pulls a little on the lead that's all.'

'Oh, we haven't let her off the lead yet, she's far too young!' exclaimed Mrs Lane.

'Do you mean she's never allowed off the lead?' I asked.

'Well we do let her run around in the garden,' said Mr Lane.

Suddenly everything became clear. Sheeba was treating the house and garden as her own private field. The problem was that although she was being taken for long walks twice a day, her owners were in such a hurry to pull her around the streets that Sheeba was getting precious little time to have a sniff or relieve herself.

As a result, she was holding herself until she got to a place where she could run free and relax. Unfortunately that place happened to be back at home. As soon as she was through the front door and off the lead she saw her chance and there was no stopping her. Then, when the Lanes opened the back door, she ran outside to finish things off. Given the situation, her behaviour was perfectly understandable.

Having got to the root of the problem I then set about curing it. There were several things to be done. In the first place, the Lanes had to understand that Sheeba was not acting out of spite. Secondly they had to be persuaded that at 12 months she was not too young to be let off her lead. She just needed to be shown where she was allowed to mess. There was a lovely common five minutes down the road and I decided to take a chance.

'Let's go for a walk,' I said.

We set off for the common with Sheeba and my own two

Sheeba was not acting out of spite . . .

models of canine perfection, Missy and Sam, in tow. Sheeba was a little playful but she soon settled down into the game. We corrected for pulling, and duly arrived at the common. Dogs were welcome and there were no sheep to put paid to my plans so I asked Mrs Lane to let Sheeba off her lead.

'She'll run away', exclaimed Mrs Lane, looking horrified.

'I don't think so,' I said, pretending to be a lot more confident than I actually was!

Mrs Lane released the lead and Sheeba tore off at a sprint, going flat out in circles, cutting up the grass and finding every puddle she could. Sure enough, after a few minutes she stopped and adopted the very familiar crouch. We left her for a few minutes more during which time she repeated the move twice.

Mrs Lane then called her back and she came racing over as if there was some great reward waiting for her instead of a pat on the head.

We went back home in high spirits where I explained the final part of Sheeba's recovery programme to Mr and Mrs Lane. This was connected with her diet and involved reducing her feeds to one a day, every morning.

I arranged a follow-up visit for two weeks later, but Sheeba did not mess once during that time and we decided that further visits were not really necessary.

In this instance the owners' ignorance about their pet could have cost it dearly. But although they were wrong to put Sheeba's behaviour down to spite they were not entirely to blame for the problem. The real culprit was the breeder. Why didn't he tell them more what to expect when they parted with their cash in the beginning? Why was he unable to help? A little knowledge may be a bad thing, but no knowledge at all is often fatal.

I once visited a house where there were two dogs and wetting had occurred indoors. Convinced that the old dog was totally blameless and that it was the new dog who was the cause of the problem the owners had the younger dog destroyed, believing that nothing could be done for it. Imagine the heartbreak when on their return from the vet's they found yet another puddle in the hall. Nobody had suggested to them that the old dog could be suffering from incontinence.

Name Prince **Breed** Giant Schnauzer **Sex** Male **Age** 14 months
Name Todd **Breed** Mongrel **Sex** Male (castrated) **Age** 13 years

Prince had a wetting problem that is fairly typical of male dogs. I was greeted by Prince at the front door of the terraced cottage where he lived with his mate Todd and his owners, Mr and Mrs Sommers. He was fairly friendly but very boisterous. Todd, at 13, was a little slower but, for his age, quite energetic. When the 'boys' had finished saying hello to me, I began my interrogation of their owners.

'What objects does he wet on?' I asked.

'The armchair, the coffee table, the fireplace, and the doors if they are open,' said Mrs Sommers.

'And our bed, if he gets that far,' continued her husband.

'How long has he been doing this?' I asked.

'Since he was about 10 months old. That's why we're a bit baffled. He was very easy to house-train when we first had him. Do you think he's incontinent?'

'No. Why?' I asked.

'Our friend had one of this breed and he was the same.

They had to have him put to sleep and they breed them. That's why we're worried.'

'If Prince was incontinent, he wouldn't be able to control his motions,' I said. 'But he obviously has control because he always goes in the same places. When is he walked?'

'Every night with my husband.'

'Does he pull?'

'Madly to the park but not on the way back.'

'Does he wet outside?'

'Yes. He lifts his leg at practically every lamppost and gate.

Next I went out to look at the garden. It was a fairly small, grassed area with a wire fence around it.

I weighed everything up in my mind and came to the conclusion that Prince had an arousal problem. He was becoming sexually aroused and was wetting in an attempt to exercise his rights as a male dog over his 'mate'. He was also obviously a little confused.

When I discovered that Todd was the only other dog Prince came into close contact with, I knew why.

Todd had been castrated and because a castrated male smells different from a male who is entire some male dogs can find them attractive.

To Prince, Todd's smell was female. To impress the 'lady', Prince therefore had to leave his scent on prominent objects. These objects mark the dog's territory which is normally confined to the garden but in this case, the garden was so plain that there were no prominent objects to be found so Prince latched on to the nearest objects available to him: the coffee table, the armchair, the bed and the door frames.

As always there was a solution to the problem. In this instance I recommended castration. At first Mr and Mrs Sommers were not keen on the idea and they expressed all the usual doubts. Did it hurt? Would the dog get fat? Would they be depriving him of having fun?

Castration has had so much bad publicity that I think now is as good a time as any to set the record straight.

It's a simple surgical operation carried out under general anaesthetic by your veterinary surgeon. Your dog will have to spend one day at the surgery and when you pick him up he may be a little dopey. The following day he will be back to his

Because a castrated male smells different from a male who is entire, some male dogs can find them attractive

normal loving self and, providing that you keep him away from mud and water, you can take him out for a walk.

Since the scrotum sack (or gonad overcoat) is left intact only you and your family need ever know that Rover has had the operation. Recently the wife of a friend had their dog 'done' while her husband was away on business and he never even noticed the difference!

In most cases, once a dog has been castrated, he will no longer feel the urge to mate and to dominate. However, do not expect the operation to cure aggression, chewing or fighting. It may stop the problem from getting worse but it should never be relied on as a cure-all.

Those against castration will argue that it hurts. Rubbish. Ask any eunuch! It may be uncomfortable, but that will pass. They will also claim that it will make the dog fat. It is true that the body's metabolism may slow down, but this is nothing that an adjustment in diet won't deal with. I believe that in nearly all cases it is the owner's fault if a dog is fat. Bad management, ignorance, perhaps guilt for not walking the dog enough, these are the principal causes of obesity.

Finally there is the argument that castrating a dog will give it a nasty streak. In reality I suspect that such dogs probably had a vicious side to their character before they reached the operating table. In such cases the owners fail with them from the very beginning but rather than admit this, they find it easier to convince themselves that their dog was fine before the operation and that it is the vet who has turned him into a monster. This attitude makes putting the dog to sleep so much easier to bear.

Asking yourself a few questions could dispel some of the confusion you may feel about castration.

- If it was a tom cat spraying up your walls, what would you do? (Remember, neutering is cat castration.)

- Why do men squirm at the thought of castration, but think nothing at having a female dog spayed?

- How long could the average man last, living on a planet where all the women winked and smiled invitingly at him if every time he looked at them someone pulled him up on a chain or kicked him for it?

- Castration does not always stop a dog from wandering, but it will stop him from fathering unwanted litters. A bitch comes into season every six months, but a male dog is in season all year round.

The treatment I prescribed for Prince was quite simple. In the first place I recommended a course of female hormones. These simulate castration for a while and although they are effective for a limited period only (in some cases they may not work at all) they will normally give you enough time in which to carry out some very valuable training.

In Prince's case we had to concentrate on a number of areas. We dealt first with the business of the lack of prominent objects in the Sommers' back garden. I suggested that the grass should be left uncut at the bottom of the garden and that, if possible, they should plant a tree or put up a post there. Prince would then have somewhere to go outside the house.

I also suggested that both dogs were walked together and that whoever walked them should try to prevent Prince from cocking his leg. When he did this, he was trying to show his dominance over any other dogs that may have been there before him and since the territory he was in was not his, there was no real need for this. Once again, exercise was to play a very important part in easing the problem. Using the 'Instant Miracle' method, the Sommers were to practise keeping both dogs under very tight control when they walked them to the park and back.

Inside the house, places previously marked were washed down in a very strong bleach solution, not pleasant, but better than the other household odours!

I left Prince for a week. When I returned I discovered that he had not been wetting indoors since the day after my visit and the family were actually starting to relax a little. Mr Sommers was very anti-castration, but I managed to bring him round and Prince was snipped a few weeks later.

What is needed in such cases is a calm appraisal of the situation. Try to be objective about it.

- It may not be the amount of exercise the dog is getting that is causing the problem, but the way in which that exercise is carried out.

- Do not lose your cool. Shouting and thumping the dog will undoubtedly make it worse.

- There is nothing wrong with a sharp word if you catch the dog misbehaving.

- If you are advised to castrate then be guided by your vet. Don't think that it would be cruel or un-macho.

- These problems rarely mend themselves. The dog will not grow out of it 'given time'.

A recent client took her dog to the vet thinking it had a bladder problem. The vet prescribed a course of treatment to help dry it up. After three weeks she took the dog back to try again. Imagine her horror then when on her return from the vet's she found yet another puddle on the floor . . . The leaking radiator has now been house-trained!

The house-training problem

Name	Problem	Cause	Cure	End result
Sheeba	Coming back from long walks and messing indoors	Overfeeding and no loose exercise	Cut in food Loose exercise during walk	Happy dog, happy owner
Prince	Marking furniture by urinating	Sexual dominance over other dog in house	Strict exercise No marking allowed Castration	Happy dog, happy owner

House-training
Avoiding messes

- try to note your dog's usual toilet times and learn the signals he gives
- avoid putting down newspapers
- don't feed him late in the evening after exercise

Stopping the habit

- don't smack or scold the dog when you find a mess — you will only make him nervous and the problem might then become even worse
- ensure that the fouling area is as far from the house as possible
- teach the dog to come to you when you call him as soon as you get him
- when exercising him, walk him to a field/park under strict control. When you get there let him off the lead to have a loose run (pick up the

motions if you are exercising in a
public park)

Territory marking — a male problem that starts with
maturity

- create a marking area outside — a post in the garden will do
- do not allow him to mark lampposts or similar objects when on the lead
- castrate him as soon as your vet tells you that he is old enough

Chapter 5
Noise control

Ear plugs in? Okay, we will crack on, trying to make ourselves heard above all the barking and howling that's going on.

- In the car.
- When you are out at work.
- When the phone rings.
- When your friends arrive (and the dog *will* not stop).
- When you try to leave the dog downstairs.

Car barking, I think, is by far the most annoying form of doggy noise pollution. Sufferers will already know what I mean: the noise is amplified within the confines of the car and disrupts all thinking. Because of this it is also the most dangerous form of disruption. However, you can put a stop to it quite easily.

Car barkers

Being trapped in a tin can with a screaming banshee is my idea of bedlam. Surprisingly, of all the minor miracles which can be achieved with dogs, this is one of the easiest to perform.

Dogs will bark either to protect themselves and their owner, making themselves heard every time the car stops or whenever people pass by outside. Or they'll perform in the car until you arrive at your destination. One of my clients had to wear a pair of industrial protectors whenever she had her dog in the car.

To illustrate the protective barker I have chosen a classic case.

Name Toby Breed Lakeland Terrier Sex Male Age 4 years

On the face of it, Toby was 'just another nasty terrier'.

I took the call myself from two very worried owners:

'Can you possibly help us? Our dog attacks the post box and we have had a warning letter from the Post Office.'

I told them that I could help and went over to see them.

I approached the door and found that Toby was not playing games. He was leaping four feet up at the door, snarling and barking in a very unfriendly fashion. But what was worse, evidently, was Toby's mad barking in the car.

'Every time we get into traffic or people pass the car Toby goes mad,' his owners told me. 'He barks and head-butts the rear windows and leaps forward to the passenger seat.'

'The problem,' I explained, 'is quite simple: Toby is a bully.'

Dogs bark to protect themselves and their owner

Toby was protecting his pack. Visitors arriving at the house were a threat to him. Over the years this had developed into an extreme habit, since he invariably won the game. The visitors always retreated; they left the house or they backed away from the window when he barked.

In the car, the owners' efforts at trying to stop Toby's barking had only served to encourage him. In shouting and bellowing and making wild grabs at him, they had only inspired further noise. Toby interpreted their human barking as pack stimulus.

I asked Toby's owners what kind of car they had.

'It's a saloon,' they said dejectedly. 'Toby has the rear seat with a blanket.'

'Then we are in luck. I have just the thing,' I said, producing my favourite invention: a doggy seat belt.

This consists of a body harness (the normal walking type) to which is attached an old seat belt strap, which slips into a car rear seat belt clip.

The dog's collar and lead are attached in the normal way. 'Toby has already spent time learning "no" as a command,' I explained, 'so this is really the "Instant Miracle" on wheels!'

The technique is quite simple. The lead from the collar is passed to the passenger in the car, over their shoulder. Toby is attached to his seatbelt; nobody turns around to see him. We just ignore him. At the first sign of trouble the command 'no' is introduced, with a simultaneous pull on the lead.

I then went on to explain that physical correction should be administered according to the 'Instant Miracle' method; that is he should be 'bitten' on the neck. He should not be praised and there would then be no point in continuing with any misbehaviour. When the lesson had been learned, the lead could be removed.

With Toby it worked very well. I drove the car, and Mrs Barnes was the passenger.

'Look,' she said, 'people.'

Toby gave a horrendous lurch forward and attacked the windows.

'No,' she said and pulled. 'I feel so rotten,' she sighed.

'Don't. It's going to work,' I replied. 'One more now. Say no and pull.'

Toby, I noticed in the rear view mirror, was totally bemused and then completely silent. We drove around the town for about 20 minutes waiting for Toby to perform again. He didn't. Even when Mr Barnes drove, Toby didn't utter a murmur. In fact, he settled down and went to sleep. Within a week the owners had released the lead and Toby was happy to sleep throughout any journey.

Indoors, noise is usually caused by indulgent owners.

Name Smart **Breed** German Shepherd
Sex Male **Age** 2 years

I knew what this little darling was up to even before the distraught owner told me. When I picked up the phone, a voice shouted above the din,

'Hello, can you hear me?'

There was a clunk and the noise decended to a low mumble.

'Whenever the phone rings or if I pick it up my dog Smart goes mad and we have to shut him away,' the voice explained.

This visit I will never forget. Smart turned out to be a very large and very friendly hairy headache whose owners were absolutely besotted with him.

We set Smart up to do his party piece and I told his 'mummy' as she called herself to do what she usually did on these occasions. We arranged for the operator to do a line check. When the phone rang, Smart leapt up, 'daddy' fell over the dog and the tea he was pouring at the time went all over me.

Mum picked up the phone and Smart, with all the grace of a Shakespearean actor, sat gently in front of her, licked his lips and set about barking as loud and as furiously as he could. Mum then did what she always did on these occasions. She fumbled in her pinny pocket and produced choc drops which she threw into those immense jaws, offering warnings like: 'Stop it now, good boy Smart' in a soothing voice.

I will give her her due, Smart did stop — for all of 30 seconds as he searched the floor for fallen chocs. He then returned to the spotlight for an encore and more drops. When the phone was put down he gave a gleeful doggy smile, wagged his tail and pranced off to play elsewhere.

'Does he do that at any other time?' I enquired.

'Oh yes,' dad informed me, 'whenever we answer the door to a friend. He goes on and on until we shut him away.'

Smart soon gave us a demonstration. The victim was a neighbour. As soon as the bell rang he rushed to his audience and sat barking by the door. When our victim came in, Smart flew into the kitchen and continued showing off.

I thought to myself: 'Now's the time.'

Pulling my battered but trusty travelling companion (a faded copy of the 'Hitch Hiker's Guide to the Galaxy') from my jacket pocket I let fly. The result: instant silence.

'Amazing,' said his owners.

'Easy,' I said and explained the cause.

Once again the dog's owners had unsuspectingly trained him to hold onto his irritating habit.

In Smart's younger days the drops had been used as a treat to stop him becoming bored while mum and dad were busy. When these loving presents were late he would bark to remind them. Gradually he had begun to anticipate their coming, and had started to demand them! His owners had given him more, and now he was engaged in an automatic sequence of events.

All I did was interrupt the sequence, thus stopping the programme.

I reset the stage and this time added my own encore: a pile of noisy pan lids on the fridge which were attached to the phone by a piece of string.

I instructed the owners to say 'no, Smart' and to pull the string as soon as he opened his mouth. Smart barked once at the phone and the pan lids attacked him. He dived for cover and was silent. We repeated the sequence twice. The second time around he lay down in the hall and then without a sound got up and walked to his owner's side. She stroked his ears and Smart cautiously wagged his tail.

The procedure was repeated at the front door with the same result. In this way we solved a problem that had been deafening for the owners and very fattening for the dog.

There's just one more problem I'd like to discuss in this chapter, that of the dog which barks when you leave him downstairs. To deal with this problem you will have to be ready to fight a battle of wills. In order to prepare for it, I would advise you to buy a square of perspex and screw it to the bottom or side of the door to prevent unsightly scratch marks. Clear all obstructions and dustbins and make sure that all valued items are out of reach.

The cure should take no more than three days (or nights), and when Rover realizes he cannot win, he will become conditioned to going to bed. If you have to go back to the room he is sleeping in to fetch something, wait for a break in the ruckus so that you enter at a quiet time. Be warned, though: you must not falter and give him a cuddle. Get what you came down for and leave quietly, with a stiff upper lip.

If the noise becomes intolerable, you must return to the dog. Follow Plan B. Armed with your bedtime reading book, (a paperback of course), open the door, say 'no', throw the book at the hooligan, shut the door rapidly and retire, leaving a pair of smelly socks outside the door as you retreat to fool him into thinking that you're still behind the door.

It usually works but even if it doesn't it will relieve the anger and frustration you are feeling so that you feel able to carry on without resorting to cruelty. One thing to remember though, never use this cure to deal with a puppy. They will usually settle down on their own. To use a shock or a bad association method on a very young dog may create a permanent flaw in his character and that would be unforgivable.

Sleep well!

The noise control problem

Name	Problem	Cause	Cure	End result
Toby	Barking in car — protective behaviour role	Owner's verbal correction seen as encouragement	Protective behaviour discouraged with drive and use of pull on lead and No as command to stop	Happy dog, happy owner
Smart	Barking at and during telephone calls	Gaining reward and attention of owner	Adverse reaction by owners to barking Result — silence and disinterest	Happy dog, happy owner

Chapter 6
Sexual problems

The sex lives of dogs can be the cause of considerable embarrassment to their owners and there is often an element of danger included too. An oversexed dog can strive to become dominant, enforcing his will on you and ravishing your visitors. Sometimes male dogs have actually adopted females in the house as 'mates'. In these cases the dog becomes over-protective of mum and will resort to growling at the husband or boyfriend when he approaches. In the final stages, the dog may even bite the offending male and chase him from the room.

In general, physical demonstrations never amount to more than a brief mounting of a cushion but very occasionally the dog may direct its attentions to a toddler or a baby.

For all dogs suffering from this problem I would recommend castration as the best cure. I have argued elsewhere in this book that castration is not an inhumane solution (in fact for many dogs I would regard it as essential) but if you still have your doubts let me dispel the myths once again.

● **Castrated dogs do not become snappy** More often the dog was snappy before and it just continues to get worse. To some extent the act of castration removes the necessity for male dominance. There is certainly no evidence to support the aggression theory.

● **Castrated dogs do not necessarily get fat** Of course there are some castrated dogs which are overweight but this is usually caused by a poor feeding routine. When a dog is castrated, its hormone balance is affected and its metabolism slows down. The dog therefore requires less food. If you follow the rules of careful feeding and give your dog a properly balanced diet (that is a diet containing all the correct nutrients in the right proportions), obesity can be avoided. Always feed your dog according to the amount of exercise it does. I would estimate that as many as 80 per cent of dog owners break the rule and because of pure indulgence, their dogs become obese.

● **Castration will not alter a dog's temperament** If you are considering castration because your dog is too aggressive don't fall into the trap of believing that a simple snip of the scissors will solve all of your problems. Castration cannot cure aggression or aggressive problems once they have become a habit. If you castrate the dog you may succeed in destroying the cause but the aggressive habit will remain because the dog enjoys doing it. To be successful the owner must also take steps to extinguish the habit.

Ask yourself this question: If a football hooligan was a regular train seat slasher, would castrating him solve the problem? I don't think so.

I believe that these myths have been perpetuated by male owners who become squeamish of the very thought of the operation but if you still have your doubts, then I suggest that you talk to your vet. He will give you guidance and may even suggest some other alternatives. Hormone injections are now in vogue. Personally though, I would not advise you to opt for these unless you are seeking a short-term solution to the problem since they are very expensive and need to be repeated at frequent intervals.

When my dog came to me he had a lot of problems but there was one problem in particular that persuaded me to have him castrated; he fell in love with an RSPCA collection box, a plastic Red Setter with a little box around its neck!

Sam clung to his first love at every opportunity, and even when prised away, he took a good 30 minutes to cool off and sometimes sulked for several days afterwards. I have never regretted having Sam 'done'. Although the operation has dampened his ardour he is otherwise unchanged and I can

Sam fell in love with a plastic Red Setter

go to bed with a clear conscience knowing that I am doing my bit towards keeping the stray dog population down.

Sexual problems

What to watch for
- marking by urination on everyday objects
- reluctance to comform to commands and possibly even open defiance
- physical acts of masturbation performed on rugs, cushions, the baby or your leg

Preventing the complaint
- strong correction
- never use the dog for mating or stud work
- castration

Chapter 7

Obedience — where others fail

Many dog owners are convinced that their animal is very well behaved and would not benefit one jot from obedience training. But before you decide that your dog is a paragon of virtue, answer the following questions as honestly as possible:

- Is walking down a road with your dog beside you on a slack lead impossible?

- Do you tell yourself that your dog only pulls on the way to the park and is okay when he calms down?

- Is it impossible to let your dog off the lead and get him back when you call if he is chasing other dogs or a rabbit?

- When you walk down the road, is your dog always sniffing the wall or wetting?

- Is it impossible to pass other dogs without wrapping your lead around your wrist and pulling your dog into your side?

If you answered yes to any one of these questions then, you have a problem. The following case will illustrate just how wrong an owner can be about their dog.

Name Zorba **Breed** Samoyed **Sex** Male **Age** 3 years

I was originally called to see Zorba because he had a slight chewing problem. His owner was a breeder and show enthusiast and led me to believe that Zorba was a gem, bred from champion stock.

She was outraged when I asked if Zorba had any other problems and I had to go into diplomatic overdrive to calm her down. But it was only after I agreed to watch Zorba perform, sit, lie down and die for the Queen that I finally managed to appease his owner. The show over, I suggested that perhaps a breath of fresh air might be a good idea and whilst Zorba was being fitted with his lead, I rescued my two dogs from the car and prepared for a hike across the golf course which was just down the road.

As soon as we were inside the gates Zorba lunged at a furry bundle who was just finishing his walk and tried to swallow

Zorba took off, pulling her behind him

him whole. Zorba's owner pulled him away, smiled coyly and said to the other owner: 'You should have your dog on a lead!'

His reply is best left unrecorded!

I let my dogs off their leads and waited for Zorba's owner to follow suit. Instead before she had even had a chance to bend down, Zorba took off pulling her behind him. That was when I decided that things had gone far enough. Catching him up, I grabbed him by the neck, took his lead and tied him to a tree. His owner immediately sprang to his defence: 'He's wonderful in the show ring and he's an obedience champion,' she said defiantly.

'Madam,' I said, 'that dog is a menace, even my children are better behaved, and that's saying something. You have absolutely no control over him whatsoever.'

'I have,' she shrieked. 'Watch.'

Unleashing the dog they dragged each other to the centre of the fairway. 'Sit!' she screamed. When she was was nearly hoarse with shouting, Zorba lowered his bottom and sat. 'Heel!' she cried when she got her breath back, and during the next ten minutes, she put Zorba through the paces he was used to following at shows. At the end of this time she bent down to give Zorba his usual cuddle and kisses and looked up at me triumphantly. Suddenly, and without warning, Zorba was off and no amount of screaming and shouting from his owner would bring him back.

Finally, I relented and bellowed 'Zorba sit!' (He was over a hundred yards away at the time.) I repeated the command once more and amazingly he obeyed me.

'Zorba down!' Again he responded to my command.

'Zorba sit!' Up he went.

'Zorba, come!' He raced towards me but then stopped short 20 yards from where I was standing, looking at me. 'What comes next?' I asked.

'He stays and then drops down before coming in to you,' she answered.

He did just what she said he would do, and I attached the lead without any difficulty.

Having witnessed this little show I concluded that Zorba had been programmed by his owner to follow a set pattern of movements which were always initiated by the command sit and never deviated from the one course. His show work was equally automatic, but once he was outside the ring he reverted to his true and basically untrained self.

It took some time, but I finally managed to persuade Zorba's owner that she needed to adopt a totally new approach to training him if she was to cure him of his problem. She followed my advice and Zorba is now doing very well in his career.

This case illustrates the differences between conventional and behavioural training. Time and time again I receive complaints from clients that although their dog responds well to their command at a club, he fails dismally once he is back home. In the more serious cases their dog's unruly behaviour has been the cause of their dismissal from the club.

In Zorba's case, the training which his owner had given him had turned him into a robot. He had been taught a lot of tricks and performed for a reward in a set pattern; sit and biscuit, down and biscuit, come and biscuit. To encourage the correct response, the owners had adopted a severe tone when giving a command and an exaggeratedly happy tone when giving praise. To make matters worse, all of this was performed at high speed and with a great deal of pomp.

In order to correct the problem I concentrated on slowing things down a little. In the first place, we removed the choke chain (his signal for work). I then set to work on reshaping his owner's voice to a normal conversational tone and introduced both owner and dog to some relaxed walking using the 'Instant Miracle' method.

To correct his pulling on the lead we allowed him to roam on a very long rope and when his owner wanted him back she called to him softly. When he did not obey, the command was repeated with a guiding tug on the rope. A week into the training we weaned him off the rope and, because it was expected of him, he came to the call at once. His show training never left him but introducing him to the new Furdiths' method taught Zorba to respect his owner's wishes and to conform to her command when required. Two weeks and two visits later and Zorba was a changed dog.

Although I would still recommend that you follow some form of conventional training if you are contemplating using your dog in an obedience competition role, remember that this kind of training does not place the dog against its original background as a pack animal, nor does it take into account its everyday environment.

The main differences between conventional and behavioural training can be summarized as follows:

Conventional training

- Training takes place away from home and the dog therefore treats the training location as the place where he has to perform tasks. Since the training location is usually indoors, in a village hall or a similar building, the dog will have no hedgerow smells, cattle or cars to distract him. As a result, once outside and surrounded by these things, the owner has little chance of controlling him.

- To initiate the start of training a choke chain is applied. It causes pain and creates noise. The dog is not entirely stupid; he sees you put it on, learns what comes next and reacts accordingly. However, when the training session is over you quickly lose control.

Behavioural training

- Training is always ongoing. It starts at home and normally everyday routines are used as the basis for teaching the dog how to behave. Because it takes place in a familiar environment, the dog takes in the smells and distractions it will meet in everyday life during the learning process so that it is never bothered by them in the future.

- A normal collar is a requirement of law and I suggest that the collar is worn permanently. It is comfortable and quiet. Because every dog should be used to wearing one all the time you are neither adding or removing anything. You are applying subconscious training all the time and the dog is constantly learning but at his own pace.

- Voice control is emphasized. You are taught to alter the tone of your voice in order to indicate pleasure or displeasure. In reality these voice changes are not necessary; your dog will know whether you approve or disapprove of his actions according to the degree of correction you apply afterwards. Although you may be able to control him with this method in the clubhouse, it will be less easy to do so in the street unless you don't mind making a spectacle of yourself!

- Mass production training is the order of the day. In normal club situations there can be up to 20 dogs for every one instructor. Each dog receives exactly the same treatment regardless. There is no time available for tackling individual problems and over-sensitivity is usually ignored. The slower animals are left behind in favour of the keener and sharper members of the group. You may well be embarrassed by your

- From day one you will be talking to the family around the dog. They are *your* pack. The dog is part of that pack, so if you use the same voice when you are talking to him, he will soon come to understand your meaning. This will certainly make things a lot easier for you on a cold, snowy day in mid-February when the wind is whistling down your neck and the last thing you feel like doing is shouting at him or flattering him for hours on end. If you have taught him to respond to your ordinary speaking voice he will be that much easier to control.

- Training is carried out on a one-to-one basis. The instructor calls in on you at home. Everybody is relaxed and the training process is less obvious. Time is set aside for looking at the dog's own temperament and your own to gauge the best approach. There is no competition and because you implement the training you gain the respect of your dog. There are no ogres, no bogeymen. The training

dog's lack of progress and could dedide to leave

programme is tailored to fit in with your routine so that it makes no real demands on your free time as it would if you had to attend classes after work.

- Boredom is a crucial factor. If your dog is one of 20 in a class you will not get much opportunity to perform. You get bored and frustrated and so does your dog so that the whole experience becomes a negative one and you learn nothing.

- Boredom is kept to a minimum because training happens naturally; the dog learns as it goes along. If you find that you're not in the mood for training him one day, you don't have to. Therefore, you will never be tempted to vent your frustration on him and in this way you will keep his respect.

- Before you attend a class do a bit of research into the background of the instructor. Find out: what he or she does for a living, and how many dogs they have trained, how long they have been operating, and what they base their training techniques on. The answers can be quite enlightening. Then ask yourself what experience you have. Some instructors are experienced, but many are not and you may well find that you are better qualified to deal with your animal's problems. An inexperienced

- A behavioural trainer such as myself has usually invested many hours in watching dogs, training them and trying our their theories on them. I have made the treatment of problem dogs my life's work and although I can't honestly remember how many dogs I have trained, I do know that even after 100 years I would still be learning. I don't have all the answers . . . yet!

instructor masquerading as a professional is a dangerous proposition and one which I would advise avoiding at all costs.

- Conventional training methods can encourage tunnel vision. Methods are passed on from one instructor to another and become so firmly rooted that they are never subsequently questioned. What is more, these methods usually do little more than tackle the symptoms of the problem; they seldom deal with the underlying cause.

- The training techniques employed by instructors running obedience classes are usually very insistent. You will probably be asked to correct the dog sternly, force it into a position and then praise it adopting an exaggerated, happy-sounding voice. This operation will probably have to be repeated several times.

- Behavioural training entails keeping an open mind and looking at every one of the potential problem areas; the dog's environment, his living standards, daily routine, diet and exercise, all are given equal consideration. If the fundamentals are put right, everything else should follow. The cause and symptoms are dealt with together.

- For the majority of operations the heavy 'force and praise' method is not really necessary. A command spoken quietly but firmly will be enough to get your dog to behave as you want him to. Over-praise after correction is to be avoided because it is usually misinterpreted by the dog as a sign of backing down. If dogs fight, they never kiss and make up, they simply ignore the incident and get on with life.

Inexperienced instructors are often responsible for causing more problems than they cure.

Name Bruno Breed Rottweiler Sex Male
Age 2 years

Bruno was a dog with an attitude problem. He would never lie down when he was told. His owner had been advised to walk down the lead (with choke chain attached) until the strain on the dog's neck forced him down and then to praise him well. This seemed to be a good idea at the time but when Bruno growled his objection his owner backed off and was then unable to carry out any further correction. The instructor who had been advising her deemed the dog untrainable and so she came to me. As soon as he had been fitted with a collar we worked to reinforce the relationship through grooming and a form of correction which he would tolerate. Bruno's poor response to a down command proved quite tricky to deal with but we eventually overcame it through the introduction of a little bit of devious planning into his daily routine.

In the first place, we cut a hole in the back gate. Bruno's owner than took him for a walk and when they returned, she went through the gate and shut it behind her, leaving Bruno outside. When he saw the hole he started to squeeze through it and as he did, his owner said 'Down, Bruno' and touched the ground by her side.

Bruno had to lie down to crawl through the hole, and by stopping him halfway through and repeating 'down', I was hoping that the two would become linked in his mind.

Phase two was a simple adaptation of the same idea. Bruno's favourite bed blanket was put under a coffee table and when he wriggled under the table to get to it, I instructed his owner to say 'down' again. When I returned to visit them two weeks later, Bruno was responding well to a very relaxed command. One week on and with a biscuit as extra incentive, his performance was even better.

The end result is that today, when given the command 'down', although Bruno doesn't lie in line with your leg he will always circle once and then collapse. With a little extra dedication to detail no doubt we could have make him a little more regimental, but what's the point? He lies down in a position that's comfortable for him and to my mind, that's good enough.

Name Sally **Breed** Border Collie **Sex** Female **Age** 1 year

Sally was another dog badly misjudged by the system. She was a delicate animal with a quiet temperament but unfortunately, where a little understanding would have helped solve the problem that she had — she would not come indoors when called — force had been applied instead.

The owners, seeking advice from conventional sources, had set out to show her who was boss. They had attached a chain to a long training lead and tugged at it using a coaxing voice to bring the dog in, Sally rejected this and struggled, so she was manhandled into bed. Not surprisingly, she reacted against this treatment and started to growl at them every time they tried to deal with her in this way. More advice followed from the same source: if she growled she was to be lifted by the chain so that her feet were off the ground. Of course this only made matters worse and when they found that Sally was growling, not only when they tried to go near her in bed but also when they tried to put the chain on her for her walk, they contacted me. Mercifully she hadn't resorted to biting but if her owners had continued trying to strangulate her in an attempt to cure her of her problem, it would have been only a matter of time. I explained that what she needed was confidence building not strangulation and insisted on a veterinary inspection before we started. After giving her a thorough examination, the vet told us that Sally had sustained deep tissue damage in her neck which had been caused by some form of choking device.

What we will do for Sally depends on how she feels when the injuries heal. Training will certainly be long and arduous and she will need to be treated with great patience, but I am confident that a behavioural approach will eventually cure her of her problems.

If *your* dog pulls or runs away you too may have a problem but, with the right advice and help, it should be easy to cure. Dog owning can be fun — it's a shame so many people miss out on it.

Chapter 8

Nervousness

Nervous dogs are by far the most unpleasant type to work with because their fear often causes them to become aggressive.

The fear of noise is a phobia that is often difficult to treat, largely because the sources, thunderstorms, fireworks and gunshots to name but a few, do not occur regularly.

There are many different schools of thought regarding the actual cause of the reaction. Some people would argue that if a dog reacts strongly to loud noises, it is because it has sensitive ears or a genetic disease. The genetic argument can be dismissed straight away because both crossbreeds and pedigrees can suffer from the same problem. Sensitive ears? Possible — but personally I believe that in most cases, bad early associations and human reactions are the principal cause of the problem. That's not to say that I think that humans deliberately set out to frighten their animals, but people fuss so much over the slightest reaction from their canine companion that they can often magnify the problem out of all proportion.

As for all canine problems, prevention is the real cure. If you spend time with a new puppy in the early months familiarizing him with strange sounds, you can soon overcome any problem he might have in this department.

However, even if you have not been able to correct the problem in your dog from the start, do not fear! There is usually a solution.

Name Jacko Breed Jack Russell Sex Male Age 5 years

Jacko had a phobia of snappy or crackly sounds and would run and hide if, for example, a log spat in the hearth. His owners told me that he was a dog who had become a shadow of his former self.

Apparently he had been unfortunate enough to fall victim to a gang of thugs while on the way home from visiting a lady friend further down the street. The owners of the other dog were family friends and usually returned Jacko at coffee time. On this particular occasion Jacko, going back on his own, was unlucky. The date, November 5th and the perpetrators of the crime, a gang of bored lower life forms armed with a handful of fireworks. As a result of his meeting with them, Jacko arrived home later than usual salivating with a string of bangers tied to his tail. So terrified was the bewildered beast that he spent the next three days under sedation. From then on he went from bad to worse.

So terrified was the bewildered beast that he spent the next three days under sedation

As his owners explained, 'To start with it was just loud noises, but now it's every little bang'.

'How do you react when he's frightened by something?' I asked.

'We've tried everything,' they said. 'We've cuddled him and given him a gentle talk to reassure him, but he's just got worse. Sometimes, if it's raining, he won't go for a walk, because he thinks it will start thundering.

The traumatic experience with the fireworks had obviously seriously affected Jacko, but it had also affected his owners. They had never forced him out if he did not want to go and the unsure cuddles and talks which they gave him when he got upset had led Jacko to lose confidence in them; he had interpreted their softly, softly approach as a sign of their own insecurity. In his eyes, they were all scared of bangers.

To cure a five-year-old dog of such a problem was obviously not going to be easy, especially as it would necessitate recreating situations that were stressful not only for him but for his owners. Looking back on this case now, the cure seems bizarre but it was one that worked.

In the first place I put Jacko on a restricted diet. He was allowed three feeds, meagre rations only which were to be given to him in a different room every time. These rooms were to be chosen at random. Directly before each meal time, Jacko's owners would have to hold their dog, who was by now so paranoid that he refused to go for a walk rain or shine, and then put him on a lead. A member of the family was then to come into the room and tantalize Jacko with his feed, although the dog was not allowed to have any of it.

The owners did not quite see the point of the exercise so I gave then a quick demonstration to show them what I hoped would happen. When I reached the tantalizing stage I let Jacko sniff his food and then ran off into another room calling his name as I went. Jacko was allowed to follow me on his lead and to eat from his dish in room number two while the person he was pulling behind him had a digestive biscuit which I'd put there beforehand.

When I explained that I planned to use this game to persuade Jacko to go outside again, his owners agreed to give it a go.

During the days that followed, Jacko moved from room to room, then from the house to the garden and finally from the garden to the street in pursuit of his food. As a result, when I paid my second visit a week later, I found that Jacko was getting to be a real performer. He raced to the front gate at meal times and no longer needed to be called to play. As soon as someone went outside or into another room he would jump up and follow them. He'd forgotten his fear of the outdoors and had taken to going for walks again like a duck to water.

The next step was to introduce noise into the game. Initially this was provided by a child's cap gun. While Jacko was busy tucking into his food, the gun was fired from another room, or if he was outside, from the other side of the house. When he ignored the sound, it was agreed that we would have to introduce other noises so we started clattering plates and dropping saucepans instead. At first we made the noise behind a closed door but gradually, as he got used to it, we opened the door and let the noise get louder and louder.

One week later and if you'd stood Jacko in the middle of a disco with his food bowl, he'd have polished off the lot without batting an eyelid. He'd made greater progress than I had ever hoped for and was only really startled by the sound of a car backfiring.

I was more surprised than anyone that he had made such progress and in so short a time. Bonfire night is the one challenge which he has yet to face but I'm convinced that if he can cope with plates, saucepans and gunshots, he can cope with anything!

'Gun shyness', the fear of loud bangs produced by shotguns or bird scarers, is very common in country dogs and can be disastrous for sporting game dogs in particular.

Name Judy Breed Mongrel Sex Female Age 5 years

Judy belonged to a couple who loved walking. She was a good-tempered dog but she was petrified by loud bangs. When she went out with them, if she heard one, she would run and hide under the nearest hedge.

'Can you get her back once she's run off?' I asked them as we sat drinking coffee in the kitchen of their large period farmhouse on my first visit.

'Yes, we walk over and cuddle her, then she comes out again.'

'What if you ignore her?'

'She will follow about 20 yards behind us and then stop if we turn around.'

I decided that it was time to put Judy to the test. Armed with a starting pistol, we set off for a nearby field. No sooner had we found the footpath and let Judy off her lead than a bird scarer blasted off in the next field. As soon as she heard it, Judy took off at full belt towards the nearest hedge and lay there hiding. Only her brown nose poking out from amongst the foliage showed us where she was.

I feared there was little to be done. Judy was quivering from head to toe. I let my hounds off for a run, to give myself time to think. To my surprise, Judy immediately sprang forward to play and in no time at all she was tearing around the field like a greyhound. She was enjoying herself so much that she forgot all about the bird scarer and it was only when it went off for the third time that she realized what had happened and ran back to the hedge to hide. Her playfulness after such a shock surprised me and I began to suspect that although she'd always had a problem, it was probably one which had been made more serious by her owners. What had probably happened was that in making such fuss over Judy when she had first reacted to a bang, her owners had inadvertently encouraged her to lose her confidence in such situations. On this occasion however, she had had Sam and Missy to play with and this had succeeded in relieving the tension of the moment, perhaps because it was the first time that Judy's owner hadn't chased after her waving her lead and shouting like a band of Red Indians.

After thinking about the problem for a while I decided on a plan of action which I hoped would solve it. It was quite simple really: channel the urge to run and hide into something constructive. I asked Judy's owners for an assortment of items; a cap gun, a long washing line, a tennis ball, a pair of gardening gloves, and a box of dog chocs.

Armed with these I set about dealing with the problem.

The aim was to convert the noise of the bang into something which Judy would interpret as a signal for returning to her owners. We attached the line to her collar and gave her the full length to run on. Choosing a moment when she was sniffing well away from us, I fired the gun and gave the command 'Come.'

As usual, Judy's first reaction was to run away but the end of the line pulled her up sharp. I repeated 'Come,' fired the gun once more and pulled her steadily towards me. She rebelled all the way, digging in her heels and pulling backwards, but I finally managed to get her to my side and then told her to sit and casually offered her a choc drop. She accepted reluctantly and after she had eaten it, I began to wander about the field again.

A few minutes later, I repeated the process; first the shot, then the command to come and the pulling in on the line and finally the choc treat.

She rebelled all the way, digging in her heels and pulling backwards

I then stood back and watched Judy's owners go through the motions themselves. I advised them to repeat the exercise each time they took Judy out for a walk and arranged to make another visit the following week.

When I went back I found that Judy was starting to enjoy the game. She no longer needed the tug on the line and ran back for the chocolate drop as soon as she was called although her owners told me that she had been upset by the bird scarer earlier in the week.

'How did you react?' I asked them.

'We just said 'come' and pulled her back. We were quite surprised because although she resisted for a bit, she soon gave in and started walking again.'

Stage two was even more interesting I decided to try a new game. Judy enjoyed playing ball when she was out so we started to play shoot the ball. When Judy was away from them, one of her owners would fire the gun, the other would throw the ball for Judy to chase. This proved a little confusing to her at first but she soon picked it up. By the end of the week she was chasing the ball and on one occasion even started searching for it in some long grass near one of the bird scarers.

Her owners decided that they could take it from there and even joined a gun dog training club so impressed were they by her enthusiasm. When I spoke to the club trainer on the phone some weeks later, he seemed quite amused by Judy's disruptiveness.

'Every time a gun goes off she races round looking for a bloody tennis ball,' he said.

Not quite the cure I had hoped for but it sounds as though Judy is enjoying herself anyway!

Although noise phobias are one of the most common causes of nervousness in dogs, there are also other types of phobias which can challenge the 'therapist's' imagination.

Name Edgar **Breed** St Bernard **Sex** Male **Age** 18 months

Far from being a barrel-carrying saviour, Edgar was a coward of the highest order, or so it seemed at first glance. He was

Edgar sat on me to say hello and then gave me a bath with his tongue

scared of going in the owner's van, scared to go upstairs and wouldn't walk across the kitchen floor.

When I saw Edgar I couldn't fail to be impressed. He sat on me to say hello and then gave me a bath with his tongue. I was particularly interested in his case because his owner had already taken him to see someone about his problem and had been advised that although common to most St Bernards, it was a condition which was, alas, incurable.

As a result of her visits Edgar's owner now believed that all St Bernards were programmed by nature to detect ice chasms! Ridiculous and yet plausible, it seemed to provide an explanation for Edgar's phobias. The van had a hollow bottom, the kitchen had been built over a cellar and the stairs concealed a broom cupboard. So convincing did it seem that I almost believed it myself for a minute, but further investigation revealed that the answer was a far more practical one.

Before I put Edgar to the test, I took him for a quick stroll. When we got back, I opened my car, a Renault 4 with the rear seats folded back in readiness. Without invitation, Edgar struggled into it and sat down. His owner was amazed.

'But he doesn't like cars!' she exclaimed.

We finally managed to persuade him to clamber out,

although at one point I thought we'd need a can opener, and then we took him over to the van to try our luck with this. He put his front feet in and then stopped and refused to budge. We had the same battle with the stairs, front feet up, then nothing.

I thought for a moment and then it came to me like a bolt out of the blue. As a town dog, Edgar had never been given the opportunity to strengthen his back legs and so try as he might, he just couldn't lift his big hindquarters.

'Jogging,' I said, 'he needs to build up his muscles.'

I set out a programme of fairly rigorous exercise, which included uphill walks, climbing railway station steps (very low, but lots of them) and plenty of loose exercise.

Three weeks later he was climbing the stairs without any trouble and was physically a lot fitter.

Having cured him of his 'phobia', I then set about tackling the problem he had climbing into the van. A spin in my Renault showed me that he had no trouble relating to cars in general and I decided that it was just this particular van which was causing the problem. In an attempt to make it more inviting to him we carpeted the back and converted it into a kennel! As an incentive, we served up his dinner on the fl⌄ inside. On the second day his hunger got the better of him and he climbed in and ate. The problem was a simple one; the van was dark and without the carpet, had echoed loudly. Now, complete with carpet, it was far less threatening.

His owner was overjoyed. When I told her the cause she was very understanding and immediately sold the van in favour of a car that would give Edgar plenty of air and a view — a Mini minus the front passenger seat! They have been getting along famously ever since although they do get a lot of interested glances as they drive along.

Edgar's difficulty in crossing the kitchen floor was simply one of grip. The floor was coated with a lacquer polish, which made it very shiny and very slippery. All we had to do was to remove the lacquer surface and to leave it unpolished. Three biscuits thrown into the room and Edgar didn't give a damn about it!

I met Edgar and his owner again the following winter

during a big freeze. We decided it would be nice to give him a run in the snow with my dogs. All was fine until we came to the river. We used the bridge but Edgar deciding to use an alternative route, plunged through a snowdrift on the river bank, cracked the ice which had formed underneath and had to be pulled out of the water. We decided that his inbuilt ice chasm detector couldn't have been working that afternoon!

The nervous problem

Name	Problem	Cause	Cure	End result
Jacko	Phobia of noises	Direct act of cruelty involving fireworks	Reinstatement of confidence Gradual acceptance of noise under controlled conditions	Happy dog, happy owner
Judy	Fear of bird scarer	Initially started by sound — owner reacted in wrong way	Distracted by being allowed to play with other dogs in the problem area	Happy dog, happy owner
Edgar	Developed fear of getting in car/going upstairs or across kitchen floor	Vehicle echoed and was slippery Kitchen floor was shiny and had no grip and dog had weak muscles in hind legs	Carpet fitted in vehicle Increased exercise Polish removed from floor	Happy dog, happy owner

Nervousness
Preventing the complaint —
- avoid shouting and overuse of force
- try to make noise a part of the normal everyday background

- approach new experiences with confidence, making sure that the dog is already firmly under control and relaxed

Relieving the problem —

- isolate the cause by being objective — sometimes the answer can be very simple if you apply yourself to it
- confront the problem in simple stages which the dog can accept and always stop at a successful stage
- find an exercise to take the dog's mind off the problem if you know that it is going to arise

Chapter 9

Dog breeds and their common problems

Getting through your own time of crisis can be made much easier for you if you realize that you are not alone. It is also important to know that when all seems hopeless there is usually a solution. To kill a perfectly healthy animal is, in most cases, totally unnecessary. If you have a sympathetic vet and you explain the problem fully to him he can normally put you in touch with someone like myself. I answer many letters from upset owners with all sorts of problems and the majority of them can be sorted out humanely and quickly.

The dog in your life needs certain things which, provided he receives them, will significantly reduce the chance of suffering the problems I have discussed elsewhere. These include:

- His own bed and bedroom, away from yours.

- A regular, disciplined routine, which should begin the day he arrives in your home.

- Your own prior knowledge of the animal that you will be taking on. Before you make your choice read all you can on the breed you are considering.

- Your understanding. You should know when to chastise him and how, and when to praise him.

- Confidence in you, his owner. This is linked with your confidence in yourself.

- A good relationship with his owner. This should be the

single most important item in the dog owner's vocabulary. Take time to build it properly. It is based on understanding, mutual respect, and care. You will get nowhere without it.

- A balanced diet to fit his individual requirements and the type of life he will be leading with you.

- Socialization and awareness schooling within your normal routine, with the opportunity to visit new places and experience new things. This builds confidence and relieves boredom. A quick wander around the block or a run in the garden is just not enough.

- Early help and advice if necessary. If you are unsure, then ask someone qualified to answer. The advice of friends and neighbours, although always well intended, is rarely correct and is not normally based on anything very concrete.

Breed profiles

I find that certain faults tend to affect certain breeds.

Old English Sheepdog and Bearded Collie

Hand snapping. These dogs are repeatedly in trouble for what owners believe to be a nasty streak. They seem to snap if someone offers their hand to them very rapidly. The cause is simple — lack of vision because of their extremely long hair and fringes. Solution: give them a haircut or tie back the fringe. I have a friend who uses hair clips in fluorescent colours (very chic). The majority of these dogs are boisterous but friendly.

Springer Spaniels

Destructive and home wreckers. A correctable trait born from the need for exercise and an abundant supply of energy. Definitely not dogs for the 'nine to five' household, these little charmers are at their best when running or working. Avoid them unless you are committed to outdoor pursuits.

Dobermann Pinchers

Widely held to be vicious animals, these dogs are often the victims of owner attitude and are, in normal circumstances, more prone to shy behaviour. Common problems include running off, lead pulling, and chasing other dogs. They can be aggressive on the lead but I find this is due, mainly, to reputation. People tend to hold them short to avoid trouble, thus creating stress and causing the dog to be protective. A more relaxed attitude and early schooling and training can help. The use of collars instead of chains is also preferable. Not a personal favourite, I find these dogs lack character.

Rottweiler

Control problems and aggression to visitors. A dog with a very protective nature, but as with the Dobermann, its problems are usually the result of a reputation which precedes it coupled with irresponsible ownership. These fellows need a firm hand and I would recommend them only to the fit, healthy and patient. They learn well but seem to need time to digest information. As a friend of mine once said: tell him to sit, wait five minutes, then watch his bum go down. A statement I have found to be true time and time again. Lots of spirit and loyal but very stubborn, I would not recommend these as pets for beginners.

Labrador

Male only: sexual problems. They tend to want to mount all sorts of things, legs, dogs, blankets and anything else within reach. Castration is the best and most effective solution. Females are undoubtedly easier and make better family dogs. Labradors have a reputation for being lazy and slow-minded. In my experience this is definitely not true. It is an accusation which should be applied to the owner in most cases. These dogs are normally amiable in character.

Yorkshire Terriers

Over-timid or noisy and aggressive — a reputation which
many of them live up to. To my mind, these dogs are rather
like car park attendants, on the small side and full of their
own importance. They are not entirely to blame for this
though. Many of the problems they have have been caused
by people's perception of them as an old person's dog, over-
indulged, overfed, usually carried everywhere and dressed
in a little coat before being allowed outside. Treat them from
day one as dogs, not teddybears, and you should have no
problems. Because of size and excitability, they are not a dog
I would recommend for life in the city. Traffic and crowds
upset them terribly.

Jack Russell

A personal favourite of mine. Lots of spirit and staying power,
best when they are working, they thrive well in their role
with true countryfolk. They are usually wrongly associated
with older owners and have an undeserved reputation for
being aggressive and snappy. Bred as the ideal ratter, they can
be both headstrong and exceedingly brave, taking on dogs
twice or three times their size. Jack Russells are essentially
country dogs. They can, and will, take advantage of soft
ownership and need a set of rules to live by. They are very
faithful within a family but tend not to accept outsiders.

Afghan Hound

Often very finicky, this dog can be hard work. It needs a lot
of attention because of its thick coat and is somewhat short
on brains. This is definitely not a dog for Ms and Mr Average.
To be an Afghan owner you really have to be an enthusiast
of the highest order.

Newfoundland

A dog among dogs, better classified as a Shetland pony.
These dogs are gentle giants, ideal with children but having

a tendency to accidentally squash them when playing. I would not recommend them as pets for people out at work if only because of their size. The coat needs special attention as it becomes matted quite quickly and ideally it should be clipped short in the summer months. The Newfoundland is a natural swimmer and a slobberer, the owner needs energy, time, plenty of towels . . . and most important — space.

English Bull Terrier

Stubborn with a tendency to be aggressive. Originally bred for bull baiting, these dogs are incredible strong and very single-minded. Normally having a dominant nature, they deserve their reputation for fighting. They need the firm handling of an owner who can be as determined and as strong-willed as they are.

Beagles

These dogs tend to suffer from a complaint commonly known as turning a deaf ear, which usually gets worse once they have been left off their lead. I have seldom had to treat a beagle for aggression, although males can be difficult. Their owners usually come to me complaining that their dog has developed the habit of putting its nose down and drifting into a world of its own when they give it a command. To prevent this I would recommend that you spend time early on in the proceedings on training to recall. A dog that needs plenty of attention but which can be a lot of fun if you are willing to work at getting things right.

Golden Retriever

Destructive when young and often aggressive in a family situation. Unfortunately I don't think it really deserves its reputation as a good family dog. I have been somewhat alarmed over the past few years by the number of cases of Retrievers, both male and female, who have bitten their owners or other members of the family. Of course I don't want to be an alarmist. Most of these dogs are perfectly trustworthy; but you should be aware of potential aggression problems for safety's sake. On a more positive note, the Retriever is ideally suited to an active social life and thrives on exercise. It is easy to train and can be an asset to the owner interested in field sports. However, I must stand by my warning and repeat that it is not a dog I would recommend to the family-minded.

Great Dane

A tendency to be shy if isolated. Truly an aristocratic dog it is expected by most people to be brave, dignified, and bold. But it also has a more sensitive side to its character which should not be forgotten. The Great Dane when young reminds me of a gangling country boy, jumping into situations feet first and always getting into trouble as a result. A lot of Great Danes tend to be very wary of people, probably because the dog's size prevents its owner from socializing it with their friends and relations as often as they might wish. They are therefore very often unsure of how to behave with people. However, the problem is one which can be corrected quite easily if they are given the opportunity to socialize more frequently since all Great Danes, both young and old, are very quick to learn.

I once met a Great Dane, who, because of an injury, had been confined to the house when young. As a result, he was extremely shy of people. I cured him of his problem in a matter of weeks and he's now right as rain.

So, if you have time, space and a selection of truly dog-loving friends, then a Great Dane could be the dog for you.

German Shepherd/Alsatian

This animal has a very bad reputation. It is often criticized for its aggressive behaviour towards visitors, and male dogs can get out of hand if not strictly controlled. Although to my mind it is a breed which does not deserve to be condemned out of hand, I would not recommend one of these dogs as a family pet. Indiscriminate breeding has severely affected its temperament and it often suffers from hip problems. However, if you do decide that you want one, then I would advise you to seek out a reputable advisory service and to make sure that the dog knows who is in control from the start. Bitches are, as ever, more controllable, but since both sexes are very powerful animals, if you are elderly or very unfit, I would advise you to think twice before taking one on board.

King Charles Spaniel

If I was going to recommend a dog (which I never do) it would probably be a King Charles. It is fairly steady in temperament. The most common complaint I hear about both males and females of the species is that they cry when left. Although annoying, this habit is not so much a behavioural problem but rather one of indulgent ownership. Because they are small dogs, they make good companions, especially for elderly people. Unfortunately, they normally become bedroom sleepers, and as a result, get far too much attention. If your dog develops this habit, you should remedy it as soon as possible, making a bed for him downstairs, well away from your own room. That way, you won't risk spoiling him and you'll be assured of a loyal and an affectionate friend.

Border Collie

This breed can suffer from a variety of problems ranging from nervousness to car chasing and aggression of all kinds so that it does not always live up to its good reputation. It is essentially a working breed and, with the right approach, can be easily trained for working purposes because it is both a sensitive and a receptive dog. In its true role as a farm dog, it is unbeatable and makes an excellent sheepdog because it responds so well to obedience training.

In the home environment, where a dog has many masters and lacks the individual care and the practical exercise, problems are quick to develop. Collies have a low tolerance for inactivity and are easily frustrated so they really need to have a very strict and disciplined routine to follow. A dog best seen following a farmer to work.

Mongrel

Call them what you like, cross breeds, cur, mutt, Heinz 57. From a behavioural viewpoint they are a real pot-pourri of personalities. The only thing that can be said with any certainty is 'you pays your money and you takes your choice.'

Many of my favourite villains have been of this denomination. Choosing a mongrel as a companion can be fun. You may set out with the noble intention of choosing a dog from an animal sanctuary but if you visit one, consider every potential doggy companion very carefully before you make your decision. For example if it is a young animal ask yourself, 'How large is it likely to grow?'

When acquiring a dog from a sanctuary, it is also essential to bear in mind the animal's past history. Some are discarded for genuine reasons such as marriage break-ups, the death of an owner, or other similar traumas. However there are those who will have been dumped for committing 'crimes' of some sort. Perhaps they chewed the owner out of house and home, maybe they showed signs of aggression towards young children or the owners themselves. Often they are wanderers who were picked up by the local dog warden. Don't forget that there's always a reason for their being there.

Some sanctuaries are very caring and try to be selective about the animals they offer for rehoming. One example that springs readily to mind in this category are the various branches of the Wood Green Animal Shelter which are renowned throughout the country for their compassionate attitude and the extremely thorough way in which their staff set about matching the dogs in their care to a new owner. They are also to be praised for keeping in touch with old inmates in case the new owners experience problems once they get them home.

However, there are as many establishments again that are far less responsible and trustworthy. For obvious reasons I can't name any of them here but suffice it to say that this type of sanctuary is never very selective so that if you do decide to choose a dog from one of these, you really will have to take your chances.

No sanctuary will disclose the name of a previous owner

but the staff should be able to supply you with an account of the animal's history when asked. It is only fair that you should know the reason for the dog's incarceration and the length of time it has been living there. Suggested areas for checking might include finding out whether it is prone to barking or to fits of nervousness; whether it has been socialized with children; whether it has attempted to fight while in the sanctuary and if it has been vaccinated. You should also find out whether you will be able to have the dog for a trial period before you have to make a final decision. Remember you are, to all intents and purposes, adopting an orphan. If it doesn't work out, you may well need to return the animal or seek counselling or coaching. If you are not entirely happy, then my advice is to leave well alone; be ruled by your head, not your heart. If you see a dog you like then let the sanctuary staff know but don't make a decision straight away; go home, talk it over with the family and then sleep on it. Remember, there's no shame in saying no.

Chapter 10

The story of Sam

The story of Sam is a personal reflection on behavioural problems. Sam, as you may have gathered is one half of the doggy side of the household. He joined us in 1986 as a result of a phonecall from a friend: 'Chris, I've got a problem. I've rescued a dog but it's turned out to be a nightmare.'

Since his wife was pregnant and he had personal problems, I decided that I would keep the dog overnight and then see if the RSPCA would take it.

At that time Sam was 15 months old and until rescued by my friend, he had never seen the light of day. He had been living in an old warehouse in his own dung and only eating when his owner remembered to feed him. If Sam upset his owner he was beaten with a pickaxe handle. Fortunately my friend came across him in the nick of time and bought him from his tormentor for five pounds.

I collected Sam as agreed and bundled him into my car. On first sight he looked so scrawny that I thought the fairest thing to do would be to have him put down but when I looked in the mirror and caught sight of the comical cross-eyed expression on his face, I knew I'd got him for keeps.

When we got home, my two sons, Lee and Clive, came running out to the car and before I could do anything about it, they had pulled Sam out of it onto the drive.

I must admit for a moment my heart was in my mouth I didn't know how Sam would react and I decided that the best thing to do would be to move up to them calmly and take Sam away from them as soon as I could. Fortunately my fears proved to be unfounded. The boys and Sam clicked together instantly and when my wife met him, she laughed at my fatherly concern and said that Sam was 'nothing but a huge puppy.'

As we realized later, this was exactly what he was when he first came to us. Apart from his appalling beatings, he had not been given training of any sort, and he had seen precious little of the mad world outside. It was as if he had been kept in a kind of vacuum. Suddenly I had been presented with a once-in-a-lifetime opportunity, the chance to repair Sam and turn him into the ideal family dog. Unfortunately, in the event, things did not prove to be quite as easy as I had hoped they would be because Sam turned out to be a dog of very little brain.

Our first problems hit us the next morning when we came downstairs. We had put Sam to bed in the conservatory, and, because we were feeling sorry for him, we had given him a large foam mattress to sleep on. He ate it, or at least some of it. The rest had been converted into two-inch pieces scattered all over the floor, except the small square my faithful bitch Missy was refusing to give up. We also had other problems: huge sloppy cowpats all over the floor, water dish upturned, and he was wearing a plant pot as a muzzle! The funny part was his expression — he looked really pleased with himself, and was wearing an expression like that of a child building sand castles.

We obviously had to start some rehabilitation work right away, so I set about giving him some lead training on a normal collar with a long lead attached. He picked this up quite quickly and by the end of the day he had graduated to recall on a long lead. After two or three attempts he started to enjoy it and at the end of the session I was very satisfied with the progress he was making. I wasn't quite sure how I was going to tackle the next problem which was his tendency to duck every time we raised an object or a hand in front of him. It was the kids who sorted this one out. They invented a game called 'Bootiful.' They grabbed him by the collar, covered his head with their chests, shouted 'Bootiful' jumped away again and crouched on the floor. At first, Sam shyed away and looked stupidly at them, but they persevered, teaching Dad a lot in the process and, eventually, every time they did it Sam started to spin round and round and began to race up and down, knocking chairs flying as he went. This was great fun for everyone including Missy who decided to join in.

I have since played the game with other shy dogs, but strangely it works better for children than their parents. I can only assume that the dog can relate to this action in children as a signal for play. A word of warning though; don't attempt to play the game if your dog has an aggressive streak and you're not sure how he might react; things could get out of control.

Over the next few weeks, Sam progressed well. He learned the basics that were expected of him and was soon walking quietly to heel and could be trusted off the lead in quieter areas. As for his house-training, apart from occasional bouts of the runs he had dried up. The problem was caused by the fact that he had been kept on concrete, therefore the floor of the conservatory, being concrete, was a place he related to for his ablutions. Once he had learned that he would be taken elsewhere for this function he soon stopped.

The chewing posed a more puzzling problem but once I had worked out that he tended to chew only those things that were new to him, and then soaked everything he could reach in a solution of alum before he was allowed near it, it soon stopped. The awful taste everything had when he bit into it convinced him that the large bone I gave him to play with each night was much tastier! Soon, the only things he was still sinking his teeth into were my wife's plant pots. This problem eventually resolved itself when he picked on one which was a bit on the small side; having spent the night with it jammed on the end of his nose, he never went near another plant pot again!

In the third week I decided Sam was about ready to start experiencing the real world, and so we began a programme of bridge and road crossing in the town. The high spot of Sam's week was a visit to the local school to meet the children. He revelled in the attention, hundreds of sticky little hands stroking him and patting him and giving all sorts of tasty treats — what Heaven!

At this point I decided that he was ready to start coming with me on my rounds. Guided by Missy, he was and still is an asset. Missy adopted Sam as her own, and as far as he was concerned, the feeling was mutual. He would lie for hours on end sucking her ears until they were quite soggy and she loved every minute of it!

Once he had found his feet he was able to deal with any obstacle he came up against. His cross eyes did initially give him some trouble when he tried to get into the back of the car. When he jumped up he hit the brakelights with his head and kept stunning himself but we eventually managed to resolve this with a piece of fluorescent tape. We stuck this to the back bumper and he obviously took it as a visible line over which he knew he would have to jump to get inside the car because he manages it every time now and I don't have to keep repairing my lights.

His love affair with the RSPCA collection box dog amused everybody who witnessed his ardour. We thought this infatuation would pass once we had separated them but in fact, it marked the start of a passion for any dog he saw, male or female.

We held a family council on the matter and my wife told me to get him castrated. Like all men, I felt a bit uncomfortable about this and squirmed agitatedly but it's a move I've never regretted. Sam is no longer the Casanova he once was and seems quite content to be every dog's brother instead.

As far as his temperament is concerned, I would trust Sam implicitly. In his early days with us, I doubted his attitude towards other dogs until I witnessed one incident which proved to me what sort of a dog he really was. It involved a rather nasty Jack Russell with a single-minded desire to fight. We were on our first visit and as the dog's problem arose only at the park, when we got there I released Sam and Missy to run about as potential victims, so that I could assess the severity of the situation. In their usual way they ran off to play, leaving me to deal with the client. I gave him a few words of advice and he bent down to put the dog on a long lead. There was just one small problem, he removed its collar to attach the line. The dog took off at break-neck speed, barked twice and leapt on Sam, growling, snarling and grabbing his legs. Sam decided to take evasive action, turning in tight circles and dashing about. I don't really think he'd quite grasped the gravity of his situation. Eventually with one determined leap, the Jack Russell managed to grab hold of Sam's ear. I expected Sam to turn on him then and wouldn't have blamed him if he had but he didn't. Instead, when he saw me running towards him, with obvious difficulty, he started to amble in my direction, dragging the growling bundle of fur attached to his ear with him.

It was then that the reaction came, not from Sam but from Missy. She bolted in at flat-out speed, caught the invader squarely with her shoulder and ran on, tight turned, and circled the little monster. He could not resist and dropped off.

However, he got more than be bargained for: Missy span on a sixpence and came straight at him. I had never seen her do anything like it before. She didn't bite him but gave him a firm head-butt and then chased him, turning the tables completely so that he eventually rolled over squealing beneath her. Then, with all the panache she could muster, she shook herself off and loped back to Sam.

Although a little bruised and tender, Sam was unhurt. From then on I have never doubted his attitude, for if that couldn't rattle him, I doubt anything will!

Index